MIKHAIL GORBACHEV

THE ORIGINS OF PERESTROIKA

by

Michel Tatu

Translated from the French by A. P. M. Bradley

EAST EUROPEAN MONOGRAPHS, BOULDER
DISTRIBUTED BY COLUMBIA UNIVERSITY PRESS, NEW YORK

1991

EAST EUROPEAN MONOGRAPHS, NO. CCC

Contents

Introduction

MAN OF CHANGE

On 11 March 1985, when Mikhail Gorbachev at the age of fifty-four became the youngest First Secretary of the Soviet Communist Party since Stalin, everyone realized that it was a momentous event both in the USSR and abroad. Following two interregnums, as brief as they were pointless, after the endless decline of Brezhnev and stagnation of his regime, the new incumbent was really going to govern and not just rule.

However, certain questions are raised: Was Gorbachev a true reformer? What sort of man was he really? Was he a strong ruler or a pusillanimous figurehead swaying here and there with the tide of events, having a sharp mind or one incapable of concentration?

Considering the Soviet political system with its legacy of more than sixty years of the Stalin–Brezhnev rule, no one could answer these questions immediately. In those days the man at the top was a perfect reflection of the apparatus, and he could not be distinguished in the midst of a grey mass of felt hats and dark overcoats seen in a row twice a year at the top of Lenin's mausoleum surveying the great Soviet rallies. Of anonymous and unremarkable appearance, while speaking glibly in the manner of a seasoned politician, Gorbachev had been allowed only to comment on the collegiate leadership's decisions, quoting the words of the leader of the day. However, when he became a leader the picture changed dramatically; he was now a decision-maker. But it took some time before he could assert himself openly.

For this reason we can appreciate the situation better today after several years of the "Gorbachev era" and attempt to answer the questions raised. The first two questions can be answered with events which took place early in 1986: yes, Mikhail Gorbachev is a real reformer who means to bring about a change in the system. Skepticism, or even sarcasm, following his first speeches, is no longer valid. Naturally his decisions are attempts at enhancing the image of the USSR abroad in order to give new life to dead propaganda speeches. But it would be a serious mistake to see in them nothing more than a device to lull the West into inertia and catch us off guard by wrapping old policies in more attractive packaging. Of course his first aim is to make the system he inherited more efficient, but he fully realized the truth of what impartial observers have held for years, quite apart from any moral judgment: the system is doomed if it is not thoroughly transformed and if it does not experience a revolution from inside.

The next question can perhaps be answered by later events, which took place in the spring and summer of 1987. The answer is also positive. It can be said that Mikhail Gorbachev is a strong and capable leader. He is even more clever and more determined than was expected, not so much because of his charm and ability that won him such praise from his foreign counterparts—this plays a part but is not a decisive element—but his sense of purpose in action, an obstination which makes light of all obstacles in his path, his resourcefulness in finding ways to clear away obstruction (by force if need be, as in the case of his competitor Romanov, and subtly with Gromyko when he was eliminated), by stealth when things have to evolve further and delays are necessary.

Although he may prove rather headstrong at times, as did Khrushchev, making people feel that he tries to solve too many problems all at one time, often with the result of making many enemies. However, with Gorbachev the whole spectrum of politics is different. The frequent "plenums" of the Central Committee are still part of the ritual, but they are no longer "non–events" as in the days of Brezhnev. So long as Gorbachev cannot be sure that they will bring things a step closer to *perestroika*, he prefers delays, even at the risk of being criticized. He often dwells on the obstacles that he encounters at all levels whether or not it seems to undermine his authority. The same philosophy lies behind his escalating slogans: from his early "acceleration," moving on to the well–known *perestroika*, then on to "revolution" and "radical reform," all against a background of *glasnost*, equally well known, and then to "democratization."

So the man cuts a fine figure indeed. The following chapters will show that this did not happen all at once or by chance. Later we shall trace the signs of this slow development; however, in the meantime, let us draw some conclusions. First, we will trace a brief outline of his career to find out whether Gorbachev is a reformer or a revolutionary and determine if his impeccable performance—through the pitfalls of the most conservative and inquisitive of all bureaucracies—can be explained, along with the protection accorded to him by Suslov, an achetype or ideological orthodoxy and watchdog of tradition.

But first a preliminary remark: throughout his youth, in the seventies, and even much earlier, at the time he was applying for a place at Moscow University or making a career in the provinces, Mikhail Gorbachev maintained a perfect profile for aspiring to a prominent position in the Soviet system. His social background is faultless, he was raised among the "new people" who know only collectivized agriculture; his grandfather was a manager of one of the first *kolkhozes* around Stavropol. Even so, his family does not include any regular member of the *nomenklatura*; his father was a tractor driver most of his life. This is an important asset with the staunch supporters of Marxist–Leninist doctrine such as Suslov, who rejected nepotism of the North Korean or Romanian variety. Those who are born into the new elite can enjoy the privileges that power entails, but they must not exercise power themselves. Brezhnev's son did not rise higher than a first deputy minister and member of the Central Committee. As for Gorbachev, he comes from a genuine proletarian family; he can and must rise much higher.

Another point has to be made: our hero was provided with fairy godmothers who watched over his cradle, but he had the knack of retaining their affection and winning new ones on his way up. Next to Suslov can be found a variety of men like Kulakov, the local bigwig who guided his career at Stavropol; Andropov, the police chief, Yefremov who fell from favor, and even Brezhnev himself, who, together with Chernenko at the head of their clique, let him gradually enter the inner sanctum of power, so far an exclusive reserve of old men.

Who could do better, and why did it happen? Gorbachev has charming manners, he is an educated man, and he knows how to conceal his real intentions. He never asserted himself when the situation called for prudence, refrained from uttering revisionist views when orthodoxy was in fashion, and was dogmatic only when tactical reasons dictated it. Unfailing submission to the leaders of the day and thirty years of biding his time could bring rich rewards in the end. Meanwhile, he took advantage of the time at his disposal to observe, single out reliable and imaginative people, and open his ears without seeking outrageous confidences—all qualities which proved invaluable when he achieved power.

One last remark regarding his career: he was probably very ambitious from the start. At least on two occasions he rejected an early specialization which would have ensured a comfortable life, but also would have reduced his capacity to develop. He preferred not to join the KGB in the fifties, when the secret police was opening its doors to *Komsomol* leaders of his kind. Later he accepted a job in agriculture, since this was in the cards, in Stavropol—but then only up to a point. He was the first to take credit for the success of a miraculous way of harvesting that had been thought out by someone else, but was quick to change his mind when the picture changed and the method was condemned. The years he spent in charge of agriculture nationally coincided with the worst crop production and unparalleled levels of wheat imports. Never mind, let others do the explaining; these failures did not prevent him from being promoted to higher positions.

Let us now try and sketch a portrait of him as a person. Gorbachev has the right balance of cynicism and dissimulation. The only surprising element is that he conceals perhaps a measure of idealism as well. Is he rational? No, not quite, for he is also somewhat sentimental. Several characters coexist within him: the man in power, the experienced *apparatchik* unlikely to take risks, if he can help it, not adverse to using the most stilted phraseology, if the situation requires it. Alongside this character is a man who expresses the hopes of an entire generation and the Russian subconscious mind, one who can tell good from evil and who is able to be irrational at times, but refuses to cooperate with the *staroviertsy*, the old-fashioned Marxists.

He is probably a keen reader of Leninist texts, but his attitude is probably not too reverent, rather that of a customer in a supermarket who can find everything there. He can quote them initially for precedents in cases which may be relevant today, but not necessarily tomorrow. His personal wisdom leans toward a mistrust of abstractions. He had to pay dearly, together with the rest of his generation, for the failure of dogmas and the stifling weight of lies.

He genuinely desires to open up the country to the outside world, since he thinks this will enhance "socialism" in the end. What kind of socialism does he have in mind? Some Western leaders feel entitled to wonder whether he realizes where he is heading. They predict that in a few years time he will discover that the entire system has to change, not just the methods employed, and then he will have to draw back. Everything considered, it is more likely that Gorbachev will prove equal to the task and do all he can to find an "alternative way." The socialist regime that he is ushering in may bear little resemblance to the existing one.

Above all there is no doubt that he does not see his position as the top man in the Party and the country His being honored as the most powerful man in the land is an achievement in itself, as it was with Brezhnev. His aim reaches higher. It reaches to the only aim that a really ambitious leader can envisage today, just as only such a man can make it a reality; that is, making his mark in history as the one who helped the Soviet Union to get back on course, who made socialism more human. A sort of Dubcek *à la soviétique*? Why not, especially as his enemies within the apparatus are said to use the comparison. Of course, this Dubcek has more resources than the unfortunate hero of the Prague Spring. He is one with great hopes of success, if for no other reason than that at time there is no Soviet Union behind the present one which will send its tanks on Moscow.

Can the Soviet System Change?

A very flattering portrait seems to emerge, but why not indeed? Several of the past Communist rulers had attractive sides to their personalities: Dubcek obviously did, but Khrushchev also, who combined atrocious and generous dispositions and is still not fully rehabilitated. In China, Deng Xiaoping left behind mixed achievements, which were not all negative; in Hungary Kadar made his best to cut the country's losses against heavy odds. Human feelings remain in individual Party members in spite of the weight of the Communist machine on them. However, this provides no solution to the pressing problem of instilling life in a soul-destroying system which simply does not work.

What are the conditions required for a thorough reform of the Soviet political system?

In a nutshell the system is bound to change, but it may also be incapable of changing. It is bound to change since by repressing freedom and private enterprise it has been deprived of all efficiency. Gorbachev invoked democracy and *glasnost* not because of any special longing for liberty but because of the imperatives of economic and chronological realities. The type of development that occurred in the USSR up to the mid–seventies—tapping mineral wealth and moving peasants to towns, resulting in extensive development—is no longer applicable. Natural resources are not as plentiful as before and labor is decidedly scarce. Besides, the present industrial revolution and latest technology require more flexibility, creativity, and decentralization instead of huge complexes managed by technocrats, which was the rule in the period of heavy industry during the thirties.

The new technology is an essential element of growth in every field, including the pride and joy of Brezhnev's USSR, military power. "If we do nothing about it," a Party man said in Moscow recently at a public lecture, "within four or five years we shall lose strategic parity with the United States and within fifteen years socialism will be wiped out." Another way of saying what Academician Sakharov forecast more than ten years ago: the USSR is turning into "a third class regional power."

There is a more dangerous aspect to this: even if the economic stagnation caused by the weight of bureaucracy presents nothing new, in the last few years new phenomena—of a particularly serious nature—have appeared in society; alcohol consumption has more than doubled stemming from an initial high level; the birth rate has dropped dramatically; deaths have increased, particularly among infants; the population has become increasingly demoralized; and corruption is rife. This adds up to an ominous balance sheet after twenty years of Brezhnev's rule. As for the culturally elite, it had to choose between abject opportunism or dissidence with an accompanying gulag—at best between a desperately grey life or exile. Russia was slowly deprived of its cultural heritage. A country which is supposedly developed and exhibits all these symptoms is a country afflicted with moral sickness.

All the same, the system cannot really be altered. Indeed it was devised to be like a rock, to resist all manner of pressures, social, technical, or human, originating at home or abroad. Only a regime without any contact with civil society could have survived the millions killed during the collectivization campaign, famines and super-purges, or it would have remained the same under the impact of Hitler's armies and in the radically different postwar world conditions.

Nothing of the kind took place under Stalin , who persisted in imposing a totalitarian rule of an abstract doctrine called "socialism," employing a stilted language that passed for ideology, and a secret police pretending to represent the Party. The system is so perfect that removing one stone would bring the entire monument crashing down. Totalitarian rule means everything or nothing. The Party watches over everything, decides everything, and controls everything. What remains outside its grasp is suppressed ("repressed" is not strong enough) or does not exist; natural catastrophes are "non-events" which are not mentioned in the press. History is more than ever a "crown's domain," as Custino said about Tsarist Russia. It is revised every day to fit the "line" of the day and historical figures become "non persons."

True enough this too perfect regime shows signs of wear and tear. With Brezhnev a soft totalitarian rule was initiated, having shed terror since it had become incredibly superfluous. Everyone tries to accommodate himself with the system, in particular the *nomenklatura* members, officials showered with privileges which seem all the more precious as they contrast sharply with general penury. Under the circumstances it becomes more and more difficult to bring changes to the regime. Too many people stand to lose from them, not only at the top in the rarified elite circles, but also among ordinary people, who are accustomed to doing as little work as possible for guaranteed, although low, wages.

The Party as a whole benefits from this, since its main task is to bring the population—through encouragement or indictment—to do what it would by all accounts do much better, that is if the Party itself did not thwart all initiative. What possible use would remain for the Party if real freedom existed? Would it not be swept away by a genuinely democratic revolution? If this were to happen, would not entire sections of the Soviet Empire, within the USSR, take advantage of the situation to shake off their chains? Mikhail Gorbachev is faced with the daunting task of breaking the vicious circle.

Of course, nothing can survive forever in this world, even regimes which believe themselves immune to change. Communism will have to tow the line and the Soviet variety is already forced to retreat all over the globe, that is apart from Latin America where there remains the last sanctuary of true believers, and it does not stand a chance to win in any of the developed countries. This is probably the situation that Gorbachev took into account while trying to control an inevitable development, warding off the risk of implosion—largely initiated under Brezhnev—as well as explosion. He still is exposed to the dilemma which Henry Kissinger described as "the two crises"; if the USSR does nothing it will head straight for an economic and social crisis of the greatest magnitude. On the other hand if she attempts

to extricate herself, a political crisis is bound to follow. Gorbachev
seems to have chosen the latter solution.

Until this time he has tried to switch as smoothly as possible
from totalitarian to authoritarian rule. As we live in a democracy,
the distinction is slight, but in fact it matters a great deal more in
the USSR than appears at first sight. Totalitarian rule does nothing
by halves; it is an attempt—if only partially successful—to remodel
every aspect of society, entering private lives as well as public. No
area lies outside its field of action, and there is no room in the system
for half–heartedness, not to mention active opposition. Stalin used to
say: "Whoever is not with us is against us."

As for the authoritarian ruler, he only repressed what he considers a hindrance and allows everything else to remain as it is. There
is room for the "harmless" in civil society, even for the uncommitted,
as long as they do not engage in active opposition to the regime. For
example, press censorship is limited to the elimination of unwanted
information, while totalitarian rule aims at dictating the very contents of publications, using the press as an instrument in ideological
struggle. Even today in the USSR, the part played by *Slavlit*, the
organism for censorship of the media, pales into insignificance when
compared to the *Agitprop*, a vehicle for transmitting party orders.
This is the main difference between Pinochet and Stalin, between
Franco and Mao. The former are authoritarian, while the latter are
totalitarian. It is in effect easier to change from authoritarian rule
to democracy (as seen in Spain, Greece, and Argentina, and more
recently in South Korea) than from totalitarianism to authoritarian
rule.

Yet a Communist, Hungarian Janos Kadar, was the first to in-
vert Stalin's formula. His slogan—"Who is not against us is with
us"—opened the way to the first authoritarian "deviation" of a Soviet type of regime. The inversion also applied to events in Poland.
The fact that this course was imposed on the Party and its leaders
by a society much less submissive to the party–state than the Soviet
Union society is neither here nor there. Only the end result matters
and this shows that a process of change has come about. It was obvious before that International Communism would never again become
a "granite monolith" as in Stalin's days. We can be sure now that
Soviet *nomenklatura* will never know again the "golden age" of the
Brezhnev era.

Indeed, even if the reforms introduced by Gorbachev were to fail, something would remain of his action. Every Kremlin leader has left his imprint on the multiple layers supporting the system; Khrushchev himself had some lasting influence in spite of the Stalinist swing that marked his ousting. This does not necessarily mean that all will be well in the end. The problems outlined so far are the ones encountered by a political system that has become the most conservative in the world. There are other specific problems of "mother Russia," a country which has always been behind the times, which took fifty years longer than everyone else to abandon such anachronistic practices as Tsarist autocracy or serfdom, which has experienced only eight months of something approaching real democracy, between February and October 1917. A country where many reformers had a sorry end, such as the Decembrists and many other generous souls deported to Siberia, Stolypin and Alexander II assassinated, etc.

Real democracy will take a long time to root in the USSR, and Gorbachev has probably only a faint idea of the final outcome. However, it would be a great achievement if "democratization" made steady progress in the next twenty years, if the Soviet economy took another lease on life and if chaos did not ensure.

Chapter I

CHILDHOOD, 1931–1950

Even in an atmosphere of *glasnost* it is no easy task to learn about the early life of a Soviet leader, especially during his youth. The only biography allowed by the supreme leader is hagiography and the public is treated to "Lives of Saints" as boring as they are distorted. Sometimes the vogue is an "anti–personality cult" and only a few brief glimpses of real life are provided—for the sake of credibility. Lenin is so far the best–known of the Soviet leaders, and all manners of museums harbor the least of his scribblings as well as his old toothbrushes. Stalin was the object of adulation for years, but the emphasis was on his "wisdom" and his "great achievements" rather than his private life, which was kept in the shadows. Brezhnev added to the exercise with an autobiography, in fact the book signed by him was very similar to his official biography with a few self–conscious jokes and pretended humility instead of exaggerated praise.

It is still early enough in life for Gorbachev so that a modest attitude is required of him with an emphasis on pragmatism and collective leadership. The natural trend of all Communist regimes through the ages makes this discretion a purely transitory phenomenon. In the meantime the amount of available information is thin. Until now the Soviet people know their supreme leader only from concise entries (a few scores of lines) in encyclopedias. For the first time a few more details have been released abroad where there is a demand for more precise information. The Soviet press agency *Novosti* provided a short description of his early childhood and his family background as a foreword to the English edition of the collected works by the First Secretary.[1] The book was published in 1987 on the subject of "*perestroika,*" but it does not give any biographical details to add to the scant information so far available.

All we know is that Mikhail Gorbachev was born on March 2, 1931 in a small village called Privolnoe, in the Krasnogvardeiskoe district of the Stavropol region. Some geographical details are useful: the Stavropol region is a large territory of 80,000 square kilometers (one–seventh of France), bordering the Northern Caucasus. It lies on the southern limit of the Russian Republic (Moscow is 1,600 km away) and its population is mostly Russian—just under 3 million. It is surrounded by other races: to the south Georgians, in the autonomous republic of Abkhazia; to the southeast the Kabardinobalkare, Chechen-Inguch, and Dagestan autonomous republics; and to the north the Kalmyk autonomous republic. In the northwest and west, Russians predominate, centering on Rostov–on–the–Don and the Krasnodar territory. Stavropol has its own autonomous region in the foothills of the Caucasus to the extreme south, the Karachaevo–Cherkess region. For this reason it is called a territory (*krai*), which is administratively more impressive than a region (*oblast*).

The Stavropol territory is one of the granaries of the USSR. This is where the river Kuban rises and flows through fertile cereal growing plains celebrated in the arch–Stalinist film "The Kuban Cossacks," which gives an optimistic picture of collectivization. Famous spas are also to be found in the area, such as Kislovodsk, Essentuki, Piatigorsk, and "Mineral Water" (*Mineralnye Vody*): names that are known everywhere by their bottles and bring to mind Tsarist palaces as well as adventures described by Lermontov and Pushkin in the nineteenth century in their poems. Even so, the Stavropol territory cuts a poor figure compared to its Western neighbor, Krasnodar, which is about the same size, but with a population twice as large and with a much higher production of wheat; the latter also has the advantage of a port on the Black Sea, together with a well–known resort and beach at Sochi.

Though Gorbachev's village retained its original name, Privolnoe (meaning roughly "freedom," a sign that serfdom hardly existed there in Tsarist days), the name of the district (Krasnogvardeiskoe) evokes the revolutionary era and means "Red Guard." Its location is at the northwestern tip of the territory, near the "border" with the Rostov region and is 125 kilometers from a town called Stavropol, the administrative center of the territory. The name of the district in former days was "the Bear" (Medvedye). Civil war raged fiercely there between 1918 and 1920. Privolnoe is one of many villages in the district and the nearest railway station is at Rachevtka, 50 kilometers away. To put it mildly, Gorbachev was born and raised in a backwater!

The town and territory of Stavropol changed names and configuration several times in the course of its history. In the early days of the Soviet regime, the entire region was attached to the "Southeastern territory," which was later called "North Caucasian territory" with its center at Rostov. In March 1937, the Rostov and Krasnedar regions were detached from it, along with all the autonomous republics to the South and East. The territory was at the time called Ordjonikidze, after the Commissar (minister) of Industry, who committed suicide rather than become a victim of the purges and was buried with great pomp in Moscow. As for the town of Stavropol, which was established in 1777, it became known as Voroshilov in 1937, after Stalin's "faithful companion," then still alive and kicking. Curiously enough, the Germans restored the old names in both cases when the area became occupied in 1942, and this decision was endorsed by Moscow. When the Red Army came back in January 1943, Ordjonikidze and Voroshilov were forgotten and Stavropol became the official name, despite its meaning, the "City of the Cross."

A Child of Collectivization

The Stalinist years took a heavy toll in life all over the countryside. The year 1931—the time of Mikhail Gorbachev's birth—saw the climax in the campaign for collectivization and a tragedy for millions of Russian peasants. The drive to set up collective farms (*kolkhozes*) and state farms (*sovkhozes*), which started in the autumn of 1929, had to slow down in 1930 after Stalin's famous warning in *Pravda* against "the dizziness of success." But late in the same year it was back on the rails, after its last party opponents had been defeated. The proportion of *kolkhozes* among all the agricultural holdings, which had sunk to 21 percent, climbed to 52.7 percent in 1931, and was to reach 75 percent in 1934.

Behind these stark figures lay a situation of intense misery and suffering, as reflected in the cruel slogan of Stalin: "the *kulaks* as a class have to be liquidated." The *kulaks* in principle were the rich peasants, but to these were added "middle" peasants, as Gorbachev was to admit in 1987. The victims amounted to millions of ordinary farmers who made up the bulk of Russian agriculture but were also a source of potential opposition to the establishment of totalitarian rule. It meant that millions of them were physically "liquidated," either massacred or deported, it they did not succumb to famine. The collectivization was carried out by groups of Communist militants sent from the towns into the countryside by their local Party and Youth (*Komsomol*) organizations. A whole generation of future leaders started its climb up the ladder to power in this way, from Brezhnev to Chernenko and from Gromyko to Ustinov.

What was the situation in North Caucasus? First of all, outwardly the territory showed great enthusiasm. As early as the last days of March 1931—the month Gorbachev was born—collectivization reached 86.1 percent of the territory's farms, which means a far higher proportion than in the rest of the country.[2] The Party chief in the territory was one Boris Sheboldaev, who precisely in 1931 succeeded Andrei Andreev, an old Bolshevik who was a familiar figure in Stalin's entourage, but also Khrushchev's, until his death in 1971. As for Sheboldaev he was liquidated in 1937 in the great purges. In the meantime, he was busy exhortating the poor peasants to violence, and had no qualms in praising mass deportations. Addressing a meeting of local Communist members on November 12, 1932, he mentioned that he had alaready deported to northern Russia "counterrevolutionary *kulak* elements." This, however, was not enough:

> Some may tell you that you have deported *kulaks* in the past, and now you speak of a whole village where collective farms can be found side by side with individual peasants? How is that possible? Well, yes, we have to raise the question of villages taken as a whole, since *kolkhozes* and individual peasants who are politically conscious have to answer, in the present situation, for what happens with their neighbors. What kind of support does a *kolkhoz* give to the Soviet regime if, next to it, another *kolkhoz* or a group of individual peasants are in opposition to the regime's orders.[3]

A little later, at the 17th Party Congress in Moscow in 1934, the same Sheboldaev painted an enthusiastic picture of the collectivization drive in his region:

> We had to face fierce opposition from the *kulaks* to *sovkhozes*, *kolkhozes*, even within *sovkhozes* and *kolkhozes*. . . . We had to fight in North Caucasus the most extreme manifestations of the class struggle, whose main characteristic was sabotage—in deliveries, sowing, and work in *kolkhozes*.[4]

There has been a recent attempt to picture Sheboldaev as moderate

in his views. According to his son, who is an engineer, he expressed
his opposition to the liquidation of *kulaks* as early as 1932 and later
joined the anti-repression leaders, such as Kirov and Ordjonikidze,
before he himself was arrested in 1937.

An Unadulterated Product of the "New People"

In plain language the local Party chieftain required his new *kolkhoz* members not only to run the collective farm efficiently, but also
to denounce their neighbors and to hunt for *kulaks*. Here is a matter concerning the Gorbachev family and which leads us to another
observation: at this vital stage of the battle the future Secretary General and his relatives were on the right side. They were all of peasant
stock, but Pantelei, Mikhail's maternal grandfather, led the drive for
collectivization and became chairman of the Privolnoe *kolkhoz*, probably as early as 1930. Sergei, Mikhail's father, only twenty-two when
he was born, was the first tractor driver of the newly established
kolkhoz. Though it has not been officially confirmed, it seems that
Pantelei was a Party member at the time when Sergei received his
card during the war.

We know nothing of whether his father or grandfather complied
with Sheboldaev's instructions, but it is a fact that young Mikhail
grew up in in relative comfort in those somber days. From 1931 to
1937, at least, the countryside experienced acute famine as a result of
the pogrom perpetrated by Stalin on the rural world. Children died
in thousands, even within *kolkhozes*, for two-thirds of the annual
production went automatically to the state. Yet it seems likely that
on a smaller scale there existed a privileged supply system dating
back to Lenin's days of war communism. The Party had to look after
its cadres and "save" elements.

As it happened, though the Gorbachevs did not belong to the
Party's cadres, they could be counted as "safe" elements, a tiny minority in the Kuban area, who were often in danger from the local
population. Thus, in the Georgievsk district alone, very similar in all
respects to that of Krasnogvardeiskoe, fifty-nine "*kolkhoz* militants"
were killed by peasants between 1933 and 1934.[5] The Gorbachevs survived in spite of their commitment to collectivized agriculture, and
young Mikhail for years was treated as a privileged Soviet citizen with
a good social and political family background. In the days which re-
sembled the sinister Khmer Rouge regime in Cambodia forty years
later, he belonged to what Pol Pot called "the new people."

What happened later to the grandfather is not known, but Sergei Andrecvich led the usual life of a pioneer tractor driver in the Stalinist period. He was not important enough to become a victim of the purges, and he contributed to the success of his *kolkhoz* where he was highly thought of by those in command. He died on February 24, 1976 at the age of sixty–seven. If his death deserved an obituary in the local paper at the time, this was due less to the prestige of the deceased than to his son, Mikhail, who was the Stavropol Party's first secretary and the top leader in the territory.

Sergei Gorbachev, according to an account given by people who knew him well in Stavropol, married twice. By his first wife, who died young, he had one son called Alexander, now an officer serving as a lieutenant–colonel in an unspecified garrison town, not in Stavropol or thereabouts. By his second wife, he had another son, the present secretary general, and a daughter whose name I was unable to ascertain. She must have remained a peasant for she lives with her mother in the family house at Privolnoe.

It would be interesting to know more about her and about Mikhail Gorbachev's mother, whose name Maria Panteleevnna is typically peasant. In 1989 at the age of seventy–seven she lives in her village and is visited at least once a year by her famous son, so it is said. She is persistently reported to be a Christian, and what is more, is a practicing Orthodox. Gorbachev has now publicly admitted that he was baptized, probably against the wishes of his father, and even more of his grandfather, the *kolkhoz* chairman. During the years of collectivization it was only the reckless people who went to church.

Under German Occupation

Mikhail Gorbachev was eight years old and attended his local primary school when World War II broke out. He was ten when the Soviet Union entered the conflict, after the German invasion in June 1941. What did he see of the fighting? Not much, and he did not experience very much hardship either. He confessed later that only in 1950 did he realize the scale of the war disaster when he went to Moscow for the first time and had to travel across all of European Russia.

The Stavropol area had a comparatively easy time under the German occupation, unlike Belorussia and the Ukraine. The Wehrmacht arrived quite late in the war, in July 1942, a year after the invasion of Russia when Hitler was trying to regain the initiative after his failure at Moscow. Hitler decided to launch two separate offensives. One was toward Stalingrad, the symbol of Stalinist power, following along the Volga and up to Moscow the back way. The other was to the south-east in an effort to seize the oil fields of Baku and threaten British possessions in Iran.

The latter offensive proved to be both the most extensive in distance (this was the farthest point reached by the Wehrmacht in European Russia) and the easiest, for it took only a few weeks, and with little fighting the Germans reached the foothills of the Caucasus, never crossing the mountains. The other ended in the well known defeat at Stalingrad, and ensured that both ended in disaster. With the army of General Paulus encircled on the banks of the Volga in November 1942, the way to Baku became hazardous. The Germans preferred to withdraw in time, and the Stalingrad disaster coincided with their retreat from North Caucasus.

The Stavropol territory, including Privolnoe and its cluster of houses, was on the way of the German march toward the Caucasus. It was occupied for less than six months, from August 1942 to January 1943. There was hardly any fighting at Stavropol itself, which was taken on August 5, and naturally even less at Privolnoe which stood isolated from all main roads deep in the steppe. The local party was at the time led by Mikhail Suslov, a forty–year–old professor appointed by Stalin in 1939 to represent him in the territory. Suslov remained one of the most important figures of the Stalinist–Brezhnev regime for the longest time, and subsequently helped Gorbachev at crucial times in his career. With the help of Zolotukhin, Khramkov, and Vorontsev, the other secretaries, Suslov succeeded in evacuating equipment and cattle from the area as the Germans approached— 50,000 animals, 950 tractors, and 99,000 tons of cereals—but failed to organize resistance networks. Only a few hundred men seem to have joined, and an underground headquarter was not set up for the territory before December 30, a few days before the Germans left.

One fact is certain, that is Sergei Gorbachev, Mikhail's father, was evacuated and sent to the front where he took part in the battle of Kursk and later became injured in Czechoslovakia, near Kosice, and was treated in a hospital in Krakow. This was preferable for all concerned. After the war, heads of families were put on a black list if they had stayed at home under enemy occupation. Another fact is certain—young Mikhail was not evacuated and lived at Privolnoe during the six months of occupation, interrupting his attendance at school. This explains why he did not finish his secondary school a year earlier, in 1949, at the age of eighteen, which is the legal limit. He worked in the fields in order to feed the village people, but also in part for the Germans, who requisitioned at least 20 percent of farm produce. How did he live through these trying times, between eleven and twelve years of age, when he was too young to do anything but old enough to observe and retain lasting impressions of the country's upheaval?

Christ Has Risen!

Every aspect of life was changed by the emergency. Though the occupation was of a brief duration, overnight the Soviet regime vanished and was no more after a quarter of a century. As mentioned above, the occupation was comparatively painless. It is probable that the Wehrmacht more or less ignored, following a year of fierce fighting, the raving propagandists of Hitler's ideas of "the superior race" and "subhumans." Whatever the reason, the Gestapo set up a special prison at Stavropol, executed six hundred mental patients in the local hospital on August 10, and committed other atrocities. The Germans were also recruiting local sympathizers. There were plenty of them in a countryside ravaged by twelve years of Stalinist practices, anti–*kulak* campaigns, and requisitions.

A clear picture of life in that area under German occupation can be obtained from the reminiscences of Alexei Alimov, one of the many Russians to join the German army out of hatred for Stalin and everything he stood for. Solzhenitsyn described at length their itinerary when writing about General Vlasov. Alimov was luckier and lived long enough to give a detailed account of his days with the Wehrmacht, from Stavropol to Berlin, which was published in Paris in a Russian emigré journal in 1949 and 1950.[6]

According to Alimov, the Germans had just arrived in Stavropol, when people started queuing in front of the *Kommandantur*, whose offices were those of the *kraikom*, the Party's territorial committee; numerous citizens wanted to help the Germans. Among them could be seen members of the Communist party, in particular one Krasnoselsky, a "candidate" member, who was immediately appointed mayor of the city. Three churches were opened, besides the one that had been allowed to function under Stalin. Soon a new newspaper appeared, the *Stavropol News*. The first issue headlined the Easter Orthodox phrase: "Christ has risen"; all the copies were sold out in half an hour, and the publication reached 20,000 copies daily.

Goods miraculously appeared on market stalls, but strangely enough, *kolkhozes* were not formally disbanded. At a peasant conference held at Stavropol in December, it was explained that and redistribution was out of the question at the moment and a return to private property would have to wait until after the war. However, the peasants proceeded immediately to share a large proportion of livestock, mostly in confusion, and devoted most of their work to private plots.

Kalmyk Deportation

It is not easy to imagine what young Mikhail Gorbachev, aged twelve, understood of the events, as he lived with his mother and sister in the remote region of Privolnoe. However, he could not have remained unaware of the collapse of the *kolkhoz* system, in which he had been raised and in which his family had played a significant part. This first shock was followed by another, occurring after the return of the Red Army in January 1943. Here is a passage from the official history of Stavropol, which was still in use in 1970:

> Only a handful of wicked traitors, having renounced their own people, had supported Hitler's armies. They were mostly old *kulaks*, bourgeois nationalists, reactionary clergymen, and jailbirds, a conglomerate which could not give the occupying powers a strong hold, for they were universally despised.

Another passage goes further:

> Unfortunately under the prevailing circumstances of the personality cult whole populations of North Caucasus, particularly the Karatchay, were blamed for the anti–Soviet activities of the nationalist traitors. In the end, in November 1943, they were deprived of their autonomy and expelled from their land of birth. Later on, at the initiative of the Central Committee of the PCUS, the unjust decision taken against the Karachay and some other Caucasian peoples were revoked and their autonomy was restored.[7]

Behind these euphemisms lies a tragedy as great as the collectivization. In November 1943, the autonomous republic of Karachaevo was dissolved and its indigenous population, 90,000 people altogether, was entrained and deported. The same fate was in store for nearly one million other nationals in the area. In 1943 and 1944 it was the turn of the Chechenis, Ingushis, Kabardis, Balkharis, the Crimean Tatars and the Kalmyks.

In this instance, Gorbachev must have realized what was going on, since the Kalmyk republic lies in the immediate vicinity of the Krasogvardeiskoe district where he lived, just across the northern border of the territory. The whole population, men, women and children, was loaded onto cattle coaches in the space of four days late in December 1943. It would be surprising if the boy had heard nothing about the operation from village gossip. He probably came to hear more about it in the late fifties, after these peoples had been "rehabilitated" by Khrushchev, and the Kalmyks and others (except for the Crimean Tatars who are still in exile) returned home.

The war ended in 1943 for the inhabitants of Stavropol. Sergei Gorbachev was able to return to his village and his family, albeit not before 1945, when his son Misha had long been back at school. Official biographies of the Secretary General give a brief account of the years following the war: 1946–1950, assistant driver of agricultural machinery in a Stavropol depot. A phrase no doubt intended to liken his career to that of the early Bolsheviks who grew up in the years of revolutionary turmoil and had to give up school early in order to earn a living.

This is a great exaggeration. Mikhail Gorbachev, who was fifteen in 1946, attended school normally like most of his contemporaries. He only did agricultural work during the summer holidays, as a slightly amended biography published in *Stavropolskaya Pravda* in 1979 admits.[8]

Even so, driving agricultural "machinery" was no joy ride for the tractor driver's son with a strict family upbringing. In order to understand Gorbachev's career, it has to be remembered that his family counted as the "faithful," the backbone of the regime, but did not belong to the *nomenklatura* of high party and civil servants. It should be pointed out that, although we are still in the early days, it probably was not easy in the seventies under Brezhnev to find young *apparatchiks* of promise who were not sons of *apparatchiks* or born in privileged "intelligentsia" circles, and this may explain why doors to power opened to Gorbachev so easily.

Apart from these two lines in the official biography, nothing is known of his four years of adolescence, of his middle schoolmates, nor of the tractor and machine depot (MTS) where young Gorbachev worked. These MTS, instituted by Stalin immediately after collectivization and abolished by Khrushchev in 1958, carried out all mechanical work in *kolkhozes* for a fee. They were supposed to organize the equitable sharing of machines still in short supply, but in fact they played a political role and helped central power in controlling the *kolkhozes*. Political sections were added in the darkest years, whose directors—more so than *kolkhoz* chairmen for example—achieved prominence in the political world. This was the case with Viktor Nikonov, who was in charge of agriculture in the Politburo and the secretariat in 1987 after running a MTS in the Krasnoyarsk territory between 1955 and 1958.

The SOVT computer (Le Monde), containing some 36,000 biographies, gives only two men working in the MTS of the Stavropol area at that time, not to mention Gorbachev himself. One is Alexander Budyka, an official of Greek nationality, who was minister for breadmaking produce of the USSR from 1987 to 1989. This example may not be much to the point, since Budyka was only twenty in 1947. He was reported to have worked in the Ukraine in 1943 before becoming manager of a machinery and tractor depot near Stavropol at a later date, probably after 1950.

More significant is the case of Sergei Manyakin, perhaps because he was the son of a Party official. Manyakin left the army in 1943 when he was barely twenty after serving for two years. He was a teacher by profession and became head of a middle school. In 1947, he enrolled at the agricultural institute of Primusk, near Stavropol, and in 1948 became an agronomist in a *sovkhoz,* and later a manager of a MTS in the Stavropol area. Was this MTS the one in which Misha Gorbachev used to work, and was Manyakin one of the sponsors of "tractor helpers"? We cannot be certain, but it is a remarkable coincidence, as Manyakin's subsequent career, which kept him at Stavropol until 1961, shows signs of the Secretary General's active protection. In 1961 he was appointed first secretary of the Party's regional committee (*obkom*) at Omsk in Western Siberia, and retained the position for over twenty–five years, in the thick of the stormy years of restructuring and cadre rotation. During the 27th Congress in 1986, though a symbol of Brezhnev's stagnation, (as a senior *obkom* first secretary, the eldest by far), he was elected to the praesidium of the congress and his region and was among the few gaining praise from Gorbachev. True enough the Secretary General cut him short rather abruptly on one occasion when he was addressing the assembly, but only to support his criticism of central ministeries. In June 1987, Gorbachev again referred to the Omsk region as exemplary in the progress it had made in fostering private enterprise in cattle raising during the past ten years. A few months earlier, in February 1987, Manyakin had been finally moved from Omsk, not to his disadvantage, to be appointed at the age of sixty–one, a pensionable age, chairman of the USSR People's Control Committee. This committee is equivalent to a ministry and guarantees Manyakin's presence in the Central Committee where he has sat for twenty–six years.

Whether Manyakin helped him or not, Gorbachev found powerful patrons quite early in his career. They enabled him to perform a great "leap forward," from the beginning. It seems that late in 1949 he was awarded, together with his father, his first decoration, the Order of the Red Labor Banner. This order occupies the lower rank of Soviet awards, and three "Orders of Lenin" much more prestigious were bestowed on him later. Moreover, the Gorbachev family received this distinction along with a group of deserving *kolkhoz* members and tractor drivers in the Stavropol area. But to an eighteen–year–old it was a great step forward, likely to open many doors.

The decoration arrived at the time Mikhail Gorbachev applied for a place at Moscow University. Did he himself choose the most distinguished unviersity in the land, the celebrated MGU, while other institutes of varying sizes located near home were more accessible? Or did his parents and other local protectors make the choice? Who can tell? But in any case, as a typical product of the collectivized "new people," the young peasant, who was both a keen student and a heroic worker, deserved a university place.

Misha Gorbachev passed the "certificate of maturity," a school leaving certificate, in the early summer of 1950, when he was nineteen. A few months later, before the harvest was over, he left his village for the first time to embark on a long journey of 1,600 kilometers across a war ravaged Russia. Moscow and its university were waiting for him.

Chapter II

THE YOUNG MAN (1950–1955)

Why the law faculty? To study law is normal career choice in western countries but is considered abnormal in a country such as the Soviet Union. It was an unrealistic choice in 1950, the year of unrelenting despotism in the hands of the omnipotent "Big Brother." At the end of the 1920s law, as such, ended in the USSR as "bourgeois law" was dead, "socialist law" moribund, and the only law was that of the Party, which changed periodically according to Stalin's wishes. The legal profession was not really a profession since lawyers were only minions of the Party whose ostensible defense of the accused was in effect a comedy designed to give legitimacy to show trials.

At the "theoretical" level, if one may speak of such, penal law was affected by the theses of Andrei Vyshinsky, the prosecutor in the great trials of the 1930s who relied on "confessions" in lieu of presenting any credible evidence against the *a priori* doomed accused.

As for administrative law there was indeed none despite the web of procedures passing for law that were concocted by the bureaucracy. In a planned economy responding to commands there is no room for an American-type of lawyer. It is much more useful to employ a *shabashnik*, a go-between and dealer of the kind that factory managers send to suppliers to get their raw materials delivered or find spare parts needed for machine production. No need there for the knowledge of law either for it is more important to have the gift of gab and above all—illicit bribes.

On the other hand, the Law Faculty was a gateway to unorthodox culture. Montesquieu and Rousseau were part of the curriculum and Gorbachev even had to learn some Latin in order to gain a notion of Roman Law. All the same, the only opening that one could conceivably offer to a lawyer in the USSR in the fifties was in the procuracy branch which investigated criminal and civil cases; or he might become a judge, whose only function was to hand out party verdicts. However, these two branches of justice were overshadowed by the "organs," as they are called in Moscow, that is to say, services of the secret police, KGB now, MGB in those days.

As it happened Gorbachev does not seem to have been attracted by either, although he was eligible for two good reasons: he was a law graduate and *Komsomol* member. It was in 1953 that Khrushchev decided to have party cadres, preferably members of Communist Youth organizations, replace the countless Beria men thrown out of the secret police. Under the iron rod of Shelepin and later Semishastny, both first secretaries of the federal Komsomol and then KGB chairmen, thousands of Komsomol members were enrolled in the KGB or MVD, the Ministry of the Interior.

Gorbachev was never one of them and his case was in this respect not typical for two reasons: not only did he refuse the offer of a career, and probably a brilliant one, with the "organs," but he also rose to dizzying heights in the party apparatus directly from the Komsomol, when it is not usually the case that Komsomol leaders rise to the top. With two exceptions, Shelepin and Semichastny, Komsomol leaders disappeared after a few years, while most Komsomol leaders' careers were undistinguished.

It is certain that Gorbachev did not choose to read law himself. He made this clear, with some affectation, in an interview given much later to the editor of the Italian Communist newspaper *Unita*:

> I always considered that my "weakness" was my interest in a wide range of subjects in many areas of knowledge. I cannot even say which disciplines attracted me more than others at school, which science I preferred and which I did not like so much. For example, I read law, but to start with I wanted to get a degree in physics. I was very keen on mathematics, but also on history and literature. Even today I can remember lines of poetry from my school days . . .[1]

One has to conclude that Mikhail Gorbachev, although keen on mathematics, failed his entrance exam for the Science Faculty. Or perhaps he enrolled at the Law Faculty because it was the only one willing to accept him, or perhaps there were no more vacancies elsewhere. R. Medvedev pointed out that out of 1.2 million students in the academic year 1950–51, there were only 15,000 law students in all of the USSR. This shows that the subject was not very popular.

Students of law, contrary to those studying science, were allocated comparatively poor living quarters. The pompous university skyscraper—well known to visitors to Moscow—towering above the Lenin Hills to the southwest of the capital since 1918, was still unfinished in 1950. It could only accommodate the Faculty of Mathematics, Physics (the one Gorbachev tried to enter), Chemistry, and Biology. The Social Sciences Faculties, including the Law Faculty, were housed in what is still called the old University, an elegant but badly maintained building located next to the Kremlin opposite the Riding School at the corner of Karl Marx Avenue and Herzen Street.

This is where Mikhail Gorbachev attended his lectures, but it was out of the question that he should live there since student hostels (*obschezitie*) were situated far from the center of town. Gorbachev lived in a hostel at Sokolniki in a building which had served as barracks where nearly 10,000 people were housed. He undoubtedly commuted by the Underground, the most modern in the world at the time. It is not known whether his parents contributed to his maintenance but, in any case, he was entitled to a State scholarship amounting to between 200 and 300 "old rubles" (ten times the present ruble, about sixty dollars). This amounted to very little, but our tractor driver was used to harsh living. Besides, he went back to Privolense every summer in order to earn extra money by working in the fields.

Little is known of the actual course of studies. However, as was expected of all law students, Mikhail Gorbachev must have practiced at several investigation offices as part of his field work and participated in the interrogation of prisoners held in the Lefortovo Prison in Moscow. However, probably the political prisoners were never there and no legal procedures were violated.

Classmates

More is known of the students he mixed with during his student days, at least those whose careers we can follow. Among them was another lawyer, a student of the same Faculty, who figured recently in news bulletins. Anatoli Lukyanov was one year older than Gorbachev and took his degree in 1953, two years earlier than Gorbachev. After working for the legal commission of the Council of Ministers (1956), he became head of the Secretariat of the Supreme Soviets' Presidium in 1977, at the time Brezhnev became its President.

In November 1985, Lukyanov was put in charge of the "general affairs" department of the Party, replacing Klavdiy Bogolyubov, who had been accused of corruption. This is a key department in the central party apparatus since it produces all the Central Committee documents, draws up the agenda for the sessions, and chooses leaders to propose decisions in its name, etc. Once called "Chancellery" of the Central Committee, then "private sector," it had been turned by Poskrebyshev, Stalin's instrument, into the dictator's private secretariat and was used as a power instrument against the party apparatus.

No sooner had he become supreme leader when Brezhnev appointed his faithful companion Chernenko to this post. Gorbachev may have acted in the same way with Lukyanov, although not necessarily. An article by Lukyanov expressing rather conservative views on democratization in 1985, and then—two years later–his ambiguous attitude in the "Yeltsin affair" (see chapter X) and his past involvement with Brezhnev do not seem to indicate that he was close to Gorbachev at all times. In January 1987, Lukyanov was appointed Central Committee secretary, which permitted Gorbachev's friend, Valeri Boldin, to take over the General Affairs Department, although Lukyanov continued to supervise the department.

Another close colleague of the Secretary General, Antoli Chernyayev, was also at Moscow University, although not a classmate and probably a teacher. He is ten years older, and in 1950 qualified as *kandidat* (M.A.) to teach there until 1953, when he joined the Central Committee apparatus. He specialized in contemporary history, which was in the curriculum of law studies. Chernyayev is a foreign affairs expert and as such worked with Boris Ponomarev in the Central Committee's international affairs department for fifteen years, first as an assistant and later as his deputy. Early in 1985, Chernyayev succeeded Alexandrov–Agentov, who had been considered a permanent fixture, and served as diplomatic advisor to every Secretary General. Academician Abel Aganbegyan is now known as a spokesman of all economic reformers close to Mikhail Gorbachev. The connection probably goes back to their student days. One year younger than Gorbachev, Aganbegyan was a student at the Faculty of Economics at Moscow University from 1950 to 1955. If they were not at the same faculty, they must have worked in the same building. It is also probable that they became acquainted through Komsomol activities. Aganbegyan joined the Party after leaving the university at the age of twenty-four. This would not have been possible without long membership in the Communist Youth Organization. Later on, this native of Armenia spent many years at Novosibirsk as head of an institute where he was teaching economics and working as editor of *EKO*, one of the most progessive Soviet journals in the field of economics. He is said to be one of Gorbachev's advisers on the problems of economic reform. Although he is not a member of the Central Committee, he was given the task of briefing foreign journalists at the June 1987 plenum which opened the way to economic reforms.

It is tempting to include in the category of university associates one Evgeni Velikhov, another academician who plays the same part in the field of science as Aganbegyan does in economics. He later accompanied the Secretary General on most of his international tours and summits from Geneva to Rejkjavik through Paris in 1985.

However, this brilliant physicist, younger than Gorbachev by a few years, finished his university studies in Moscow three years later and qualified for a place in the new building on the Lenin Hills. The connection is more obvious in the case of art students such as Anatoli Adamishin, who left the University in 1957 and is now deputy-minister of Foreign Affairs, or Alexander Kamshalov, who attended the History Faculty until 1951 and is today chairman of the state committee for the cinema, the Goskino. Here the connection with Gorbachev is probable, as Kamshalov worked as a permanent Komsomol official immediately after graduation and was appointed to his present position in December of 1986, at the time of Gorbachev's drive for restructuring culture.

Of course, university and Komsomol links work both ways. Another university companion in the years 1950–55 was Richard Kosolapov. Like Gorbachev he became Komsomol leader in the provinces (Bryansk), but wanted to be an ideologist and theoretician, the fastest way to rise in party hierarchy. Kosolapov was a teacher and researcher at thirty, became second–in–command on the editorial board of *Pravda* in 1974, later editor–in–chief of the official Party monthly *Komunist* for ten years. However, Kosolapov became eminent during the Brezhnev era of conservatism, later labeled "stagnation." In February 1986 he was fired from his job and replaced by Ivan Frolov, a less rigid philosopher and later one of Gorbachev's personal assistants.

A Foreign Friend: Zdenek Mlynar

There were others besides Soviet students in Gorbachev's circle of acquaintances. Since 1950, and more so after Stalin's death, Moscow University took in foreign students—not just anyone, of course, but nationals of countries belonging to what was humorously called the socialist "camp." First of all, the Chinese were the most numerous, since China was a staunch ally at the time and the most hard working as well, but they preferred to keep to themselves. (Mao had personally forbidden them any flirtation or marriage with Russian colleagues.) Next came students from Eastern Europe, the people's democracies, who were supposed to love the great Soviet Union dearly, emulating her in every way.

One of these students was Zdenek Mlynar, a Czech, who attended the old university between 1950 and 1955, like Gorbachev, and boarded in the same Sokolniki hostel. He was more of a "real lawyer" than Gorbachev, for upon his return to Prague he became assistant to the Czechoslovak Attorney General. It was only later that he became involved in politics to be swept away after August 1968. He was the youngest secretary of the Czechoslovak Communist Party. In the Prague Spring, he was in favor of reforms which brought his downfall soon after Russian tanks had entered Prague, even before Dubcek. A few years later he was forced to settle in Vienna.

Success attracts attention, and so keen were Gorbachev's biographers to find a "witness," (combined with a mistake in translating an article written by Mlynar for *Units* in 1985), that they made the Czech share a bedroom with Mikhail Gorbachev.[2] Another remarkable coincidence was Mlynar's choice of subject for his dissertation: "Machiavelli and his Conception of Power." It is tempting to suggest that the man who is master in the Kremlin read *The Prince* and other heretical books lent to him by his roommate. Alas, there is no evidence for this. Mlynar himself told me that they had not shared bedrooms. As for Machiavelli, the ex–Czech party official did acknowledge it was the subject chosen for his thesis and that he and Gorbachev had discussed it on occasion. However, he had no idea of what impression this had made upon him.

What is certain is that Mlynar was one of the closest university friends of the future Secretary General. They met again later, at least once, in 1967. Mlynar's memories are bound to suffer from some reticence and may seem one–sided (a few anecdotes would have been

welcome), but they are interesting. The full version was published by
the monthly *L'Autre Europe*:

> We attended the same tutorials, prepared our exams to-
> gether and got our qualifications in the same year, both with
> distinction. We were more than classmates; they all looked
> upon us as friends. . . . Gorbachev was an extrovert,
> never showed signs of arrogance and was highly intelligent.
> He was willing to listen and learn from others. He was an
> honest man, a man of good will, enjoying real authority, as
> opposed to bullying, although he was not without pride. .
> . . Gorbachev never showed a trace of cynicism, but was a
> natural reformer. . . . Once he told me that "Lenin did
> not send Martov (a Menshevik leader who opposed him) to
> jail, he allowed him to emigrate." In 1952, this meant that
> Gorbachev, a law student, doubted that people could be di-
> vided between those who towed the party line while others
> were criminals.

Admittedly, from 1952 as a Komsomol leader and party member,
Gorbachev had to be careful with "honesty" and "compassion," in his
comments on recent events, particularly on the "doctors' plot" early
in 1953. It is true that exchanging ideas with a comrade from a
country which, although orthodox, since it had only recently become
communist and was still imbued with western thought and democratic
tradition was frowned upon. This must have been stimulating for an
"open-minded and inquisitive" student fresh from Stavropol, all the
more so since Mlynar remained the only foreigner he met for a long
time. In his words:

> I was the first foreigner that Gorbachev had come across in
> real life. In 1951, I sent a post card to him to his village from
> Prague. During summer vacations, Gorbachev went home
> and worked with a combine harvester. He later told me how
> this card was delivered. The chief constable came to him
> in the fields to hand over this suspicious thing—a post card
> from abroad. We had a good laugh over it.[3]

They laughed, but it should be mentioned that Gorbachev was
cautious enough not to reply, since Mlynar would certainly have told
us if there had been an answer. Later on, this friendship proved to
be embarrassing. When Bettino Craxi, the Italian Prime Minister
of the day, asked him about it, Gorbachev admitted he knew Mlynar, but refused to go into detail. At a time when his enemies were

watching him because of his reforming zeal, already referring to him as the "Soviet Dubcek," it was unwise to parade a friendship with a "revisionist" of the Prague Spring.

Raisa

The charming personality which had endeared Gorbachev to his Czech fellow student soon conquered another person of greater significance. Raisa Gorbachev is known all over the world as a traveling companion of her husband during his trips abroad where she exerted her charms upon such people as Margaret Thatcher, Radjiv Gandhi, Ronald Reagan, and Danielle Mitterrand—although by all accounts she was not so charming with Nancy Reagan. Her pleasant appearance contrasts sharply with the imposing presence of the matrons who accompanied Brezhnev—though infrequently—or Chernenko. She attends fashion shows and goes shopping in Western European countries. However, little is known of her background and life story.

Mlynar tells us very little:

> Gorbachev met his wife when they were university students. Raisa Titorenko was reading philosophy, so that she attended classes in the same building of the old university where social sciences were taught, and she lived in the same hostel as we did.[4]

Beyond that, the picture is rather vague. Only later did Gorbachev mention that he met Raisa in 1951 and that they were married in 1953. Their only child, Irina, was born in 1956. According to Alexander Rahr, the young couple was able to leave the students' hostel to live in a small flat on the Moscow causeway, located rather far from the center, but a place they could call their own.

The official news is that Raisa Maximovna Titorenko was born on January 5, 1932 in the city of Rubtsoosk, in the Altai, and that both her parents now live at Rostov-on-the-Don. Her father, a Ukrainian, as determined by his name, was working in the railway system. Rumor has it that he was arrested under Stalin and spent two years in the Gulag, in the very camp where Academician Dimitri Likhachev was interned. He is now a chairman of the Soviet Culture Fund of which Raisa is one of the most eminent patrons. What a small world!

Other rumors saying that Raisa was a niece of Andrei Gromyko can be discarded though they would have provided for the budding

Secretary General with another sponsor, the perennial Foreign Minister. In reality Gromyko, by his own admission, had one sister, Evdokia Andreyevna, a Byelorussian like himself, who never lived in the Donetz.[5] Besides, Arkady Shevchenko, who writes at length about Gromyko and Gorbachev, would have mentioned the family ties, had there been any.

The Stavropol Sociologist

The photographs of Raisa seen in the world press, along with a few comments of hers published in newspapers, tell us next to nothing of her achievements as a philosopher, her contributions as a sociologist and her personality. The one fact available is that, in 1967, while her husband was already First Party Secretary in the city of Stavropol, Raisa defended her thesis, a copy of which is retained in the Lenin Library in Moscow under the impressive title of "The Emergence of New Characteristics in the World of Kolkhoz Peasantry. Results of sociological enquiry in the Stavropol district."

I have not read the thesis, but an American academic, William Shinn, obtained the book published by Raisa two years later where she used the material in her thesis for an article. Fifteen hundred copies of the book were printed by a Stavropol printer. For the first time the USSR opinion polls were used by a researcher when Raisa sent several thousand forms to agricultural workers employed in six different *kolkhozes* in the area with questions concerning their daily lives. She received 3,130 replies and interviewed a number of people. What were her conclusions? This is what William Shinn writes:

> Raisa Maximova writes in a decidedly dogmatic and didactic fashion. She wants to prove that the standard of living of the Russian peasant rose constantly since 1917. She mentions in passing the years of collectivization, but does not write a word about Stalin. . . . She is undoubtedly ideologically biased, praising the urban type of dwelling and downgrading the traditional farmhouse. . . . Strongly in favor of feminism, she supports communal kitchens, to relieve peasant women of the chores of cooking. After attacking God Almighty for the legend of Adam and Eve, . . . she advocates a switch from religious ceremonies to more "enlightened" ones.[6]
>
> She is essentially a conformist, but shows a measure of objec-

tivity since she remarks that "half of the families in three out of six of the villages under scrutiny revealed that they celebrated Easter, Christmas, Trinity Sunday, and a few other festivals." William Shinn continues:

> Raisa Gorbacheva is worried by people answering that their main pastime is drinking in the company of friends. Card games and dominoes come soon after that. Raisa thinks this latter game a particularly pernicious occupation, for she sees it as "one that in no way contributes to a better spiritual life." She values highly reading, theater going, and cinema as a form of entertainment, which open the mind to good work and creative activities. . .[7]

All of this is in keeping with the doctrine favored by official ideologists. Raisa was slightly odd when appearing indignant about the story of Adam and Eve or the game of dominoes. By now, undoubtedly, she has become more realistic, particularly since her travels abroad. Curiously enough her research and the book it was based on were written after an early trip the Gorbachevs made to the French countryside, as will be seen below.

It is significant all the same that Gorbachev married a person of the same level of education, which sets him apart from all the other Secretaries General since Stalin. His wife could discuss anything with him and air points of view on any subject, in particular philosophy with some sophistication. Raisa spent many long years in the provinces as a philosophy teacher in the Stavropol Teacher Training Institute.

Komsomol Years

In the meantime Gorbachev's profile as a politician was becoming sharper. There is no doubt that he saw in his activities a springboard to a career in politics. Zdenek Mlynar recalls: "One could tell that his ambition was not a career as an investigating magistrate, like most of us, but that he set his sights higher." The safest way up for one with an advantage of a faultless past in collective farming was to enroll in the Communist Youths, the Komsomol. Even better, since students had the right of entry to the organization, which gave them access to membership in the Party, to later become a leader.

So Mikhail Gorbachev enrolled in the Komsomol at the start of the academic year 1950. His official biographers state that only in 1952 did he become "Komsomol organizer" (*komsorg*) at the Law Faculty, when he was already a full Party member. The position was not very exalted; he was responsible for the students attending his course of studies, which gave him a seat on the Faculty Komsomol board in charge of other courses, joining ten other students.

Some old University students, who now live in exile in West Germany, believe even this humble achievement was not easy for him to achieve. Some have it that a student, called Nikitin, had been elected at first, but then he was caught staggering about in an advanced stage of intoxication. At the next meeting, Mikhail Gorbachev attacked this behavior and was elected as *komsorg*. Later on, Gorbachev's position became even more difficult. Alexander Rahr, on the strength of certain reports, gives the following account:

> [Gorbachev] suffered a bitter defeat in the summer of 1954. He was deprived of his position as Komsomol secretary of the Law Faculty at Moscow University in favor of Kondratenko, a student who had just been demobilized. What was the reason for it? After the merger of Moscow University Law Faculty with the Moscow Law Institute, the balance of power in the Komsomol leadership of the faculty had radically altered. The Law Institute was in the hands of an internal clique of war veterans. Through clever maneuvering the *frontoviki*, as they were called, won strong support from the Moscow City party apparatus. Gorbachev's career at the University had come to an end.

This version is in contradiction with the official biography, which states that Mikhail Gorbachev remained a *komsorg* until he graduated in 1955. The emigrés' stories should be taken with caution as their rememberance of a minor *komsorg* may be somewhat hazy. Even so, the opposition within the University between "ordinary" students and soldiers who had just returned from the front was a fact to which more trustworthy accounts bear witness, like those of Medvedev or Mlynar. It seems likely that the more enterprising among the veterans, eager to secure for themselves the good Party posts in Moscow, were prepared to push humble civilians out of the way.

Mikhail Gorbachev may have worn under his lapel the Red Banner of Labor, a decoration which he had earned driving a combine–harvester, but he was no match for the heroes of Stalingrad and Berlin.

Another element tends to corroborate the hypothesis of Gorbachev's defeat in this early contest for power. The leaders who ousted him at the Law Faculty must have sat on the Moscow City Komsomol committee, or even on the City Party committee. A quick glance through the list of persons on the two bodies shows that several of them fell into disgrace under Brezhnev, but their fate was finally sealed on Gorbachev's assumption of the Party leadership in 1985.

A member of the Moscow apparatus who was on the Komsomol committee at the time, Sergei Pavlov—an ambitious man slightly older than Gorbachev—became head of the Komsomol organization for the entire country in 1959. He first fell from favor in 1968 because of his connection with Shelepin; he was downgraded to the State Committee for Sports and in 1971 lost his seat on the Central Committee. On Brezhnev's death he was "exiled," first as ambassador to Mongolia (February 1983), and later to Burma (July 1985), which meant that he lost his seat on the Central Revison Commission in 1986.

In a similar fashion Alexander Subbotin, who served as chief editor of *Moskovsky Komsomolets* between 1951 and 1958, lost his position in February 1987 as secretary of the Central Trade Unions Council at the age of sixty-five. Mikhail Khaldeyev, first secretary of the Moscow Komsomol committee between 1952 and 1953 fared better. Although he is over sixty-six, he has remained as chief editor of the journal *The Party Life* for more than twenty years. It may be due to the fact that he bore no responsibility for the Law Faculty "defeat" which occurred in 1954.

The same sort of problems crop up in the careers of Party Committee members in those days. The chief personality was Yekaterina Furtseva, second secretary, until the spring of 1954, first secretary thereafter. A close friend of Khrushchev, Furteseva died in 1974, but her two deputies, who are still alive, did not survive Gorbachev's ascent to power: Vasili Prokhorov, secretary and later deputy chairman of the Soviet Trade Unions Council for thirty years, and Vladimir Promyslov, the unmovable Mayor of Moscow in Brezhnev's days. The former was retired one month after Gorbachev became Secretary General (he was nearly eighty years old), the latter was sacked with his reputation tarnished soon after his associate and patron Viktor Grichin fell.

On the other hand, the first secretary, who witnessed Gorbachev's early steps in politics and who had left the capital a few months before the clash at the Law Faculty, was given advancement regardless.

Ivan Kapitonov was secretary of the Central Committee where he was responsible for cadres for over twenty years. In 1986, at the age of seventy–one, he was granted a comfortable position as head of the Central Revision Commission. Gorbachev acknowledged services rendered in this way and reciprocated, as will be shown below—one more Stalinist in the family.

In 1952, as *komsorg*, Mikhail Gorbachev joined the "Communist (Bolshevik) Party of the USSR," as it was then called. At least this is an official date of membership, although he had already taken steps to become a candidate member in 1951, which was a probational period when he attended the cell meetings without a right to vote.

A Soviet youth, communist party member in 1952, and thirty-three years later the supreme leader requires a faultless run in the party apparatus, and is a culmination of a carefully planned career. However, the rise was not easy, especially for a man of Gorbachev's generation.

I came to know a number of people of that generation, those who were born in the thirties, when I first visited Moscow in 1957, and subsequently as well. They had worked slowly into the world of politics after a rigorous education in Stalinism. This was no longer the dead silent era of their parents, terrified by the purges (not much had been heard about them by the children), but an era of cozy certainties, engendered by the difficult and undramatic postwar conditions. Much later, middle–aged men would feel nostalgic about these days of simple academic work and friendship, factory festivals, and the protective shadow of "*kollective*" life, when vodka was cheap and food prices fell every year, and they were lulled by Stalin's declarations into a false feeling of security. The "*vezhd*" (the boss) saw to everything. There was no need to worry about him or politics, since he was there to take care everything and would remain there forever.

In politics, since they lived in a system—supposedly the best in the world—where nothing ever happened, no news was good news. The most painstaking historians cannot find in the limbs of the early 1950s anything remarkable happening. In 1949 there did occur a purge of almost every party leader in Leningrad but, unlike the 1930s, there was no trial nor press report. Nonetheless a politburo member, Voznesensky, fell into disgrace, unnoticed. Stalin, probably out of boredom, suddenly made a foray into linguistics. He published in *Pravda* an article in which he criticized the assertions of Marr, a linguist long dead, who in the 1920s had paradoxically made a name as a defender of Stalinism in linguistics, just as Lysenko was doing in a similar way in biology. For once Stalin was fighting for a just cause, but who cared?

One year later, the "strategist of genius" published another major work in 1952, *The Economic Problems of Socialism*, which was acclaimed as the epitome of Marxist thought by Communists the world over. Students did hear of it, since the collected aphorisms were at the center of their innumerable classes in "*diamat*" (dialectical materialism) if it was not "*istmat*" (historical materialism). Some time later, the 19th Party Congress, in October 1952, saw Stalin's last public appearances and another expression of the personality cult. The account given by *Pravda* of his short speech is interspersed with reports of "standing ovations" and chanted slogans which accompanied it.

This was the moment—at the age of twenty–one—of Gorbachev becoming a full member of the Communist party. Another Stalinist in the family? No doubt, and he will have to show it fairly soon. Early in 1953, the "doctors' plot" was announced. In the version imagined by Stalin (not by Beria, head of the political police, who was somewhat in disfavor), it was determined that a group of doctors who looked after the leaders' health had decided to murder them. A few years earlier they had started with Zhdanov, previously the party boss in Leningrad and later in charge of ideology, who had in effect died under suspicious circumstances in August 1948. The accusation rested on the confession of those concerned, as in the great trials of the 1930s, and confession was used as evidence for the first time since then.

How did Gorbachev feel at the time? Mlynar, along with other Moscow University students who were not living in exile, thought—although without giving precise details—that the Komsomol leader looked calm during the meetings when they examined the "private lives" of the unfortunate plotters.

It is clear that in a matter of such political importance as the "doctors' plot," Gorbachev followed the Party line. The propaganda machine was well oiled, casting anathemas on the "murders in white blouses," not only in the USSR but also among Communist parties abroad. The affair was exploited for another anti–Semitic campaign (most of the doctors implicated were Jewish). Anti–Semitism had been simmering since the 1930s and had flared up with the arrest of Jewish intellectuals in 1948. It is highly probable that the local Komsomol leader made the required speeches against "cosmopolitanism," "medical traitors," and "corrupt liberalism" to comply with the Party campaign. What went on in Gorbachev's mind at the time? We may never know. Only his deeds and words are relevant to the story, but this painful episode can be seen as an early example of the kind of schizophrenic behavior that went hand in hand with a career in the Party.

From then on, events followed rapidly one upon the other. Two months later, Stalin died. It is probable that Mikhail Gorbachev took part in the burial ceremonies like every other inhabitant of the capital at the time. This was more in deference to history than to the personality cult. Those who were young at the time remember an enormous crush in which hundreds of people died and the general feeling of helplessness after the "Father" had vanished. On the other hand there was no time for a long mourning period, since a series of revelations threw a new light on Stalin's public life.

First of all, the "guilty" doctors were rehabilitated, which cast a serious doubt on many previous trials and shattered the legal basis of the past twenty years of repression. Then came Beria's downfall. Since he was much more in the public eye than Voznesenski in 1949, when his portraits suddenly vanished in June 1953, everyone was flabbergasted. Children started to chant this rhyme:

Tovaritch Malenkov nam dal khleb i blinkov

A tovaritch Beria ne opravdal doveriia.

(Comrade Malenkov has given us bread and pancakes

But Comrade Beria does not deserve confidence.)

The adult population saw the year 1953 as emerging from Stalin's inferno. They became more politically conscious and experienced a growing feeling of disappointment with the evolution of the new regime. Millions of deportees who described conditions in camps returned home. The 20th Congress, a first stage in destalinization, as well as the rebellions in Hungary and Poland, followed. Later there was the political crises of the "anti–party group," which ended in 1957 with the ouster of Molotov, Malenkov, Kaganovich, and others from the politburo (then called the presidium of the Central Committee). In 1964 came the fall of Khrushchev, the new dictator. All these somersaults were enough to make people skeptical about politics. The new situation was a lesson for every Soviet citizen, especially for those who were to become political leaders, on how to interpret a world more unstable though still fairly rigid and how to conform to a party line of the moment while planning to build a better system.

This may be what Mikhail Gorbachev had in mind when—as a qualified lawyer and Party member with an appointment from the Komsomol in his pocket—he boarded the train to Stavropol on a summer's day in 1955 when he set out to settle there with his new wife. Was he satisfied with this job, or did he nurse a grievance for losing the battle against the "*frontoviki*" at the Law Institute? As one of the ex–students at Moscow University, the writer Neznanski remarked, if Gorbachev had not been obliged to go back to the provinces after graduation, "who knows whether he would have risen higher than professor of Marxism–Leninism? Competition in Moscow was so harsh."[8] In reality, it took him twenty years to return to the capital city. But it was then that all the doors of power were wide open.

Chapter III

APPARATCHIK (1955–1978)

To understand the faultless run lasting twenty–three years made by Mikhail Gorbachev as an *apparatchik*, it is essential to know a little of Soviet institutions as they were until 1989.

Generallly speaking, the Party structure is the same at all levels, be it the *raion* (borough), *gorod* (town) region or territory (*oblast* or *krai*). Above them are the republics. Since Stavropol belongs to the Federal Russian Republic (RSFSR), the largest and the least "structured" of the fifteen Soviet Republics, the territory depends directly, similar to all its other regions, on the Central Committee of the Soviet Communist Party.

At all levels assemblies gather regularly where conventions or congresses take place. They elect smaller committees, and those in turn appoint executive organs to wield power. The latter consist of three bodies: a bureau (smaller than the committees); a secretariat (varying in size according to the geographic echelon) invariably under the authority of a first secretary; and service departments which are the backbone of the secretariat and make up the celebrated apparatus. The first secretary of the *obkom* (short for regional committee) is the undisputed master in the region, followed by the first secretary of the *kraikom* in the territory, the first secretary of *gorkom* in a town, and so forth.

At all levels, the Party leaders have to deal with the executive apparatus: for example, with an executive committee for a territory (*kraispolkom*, the equivalent of a regional council) and its chairman; an executive committee for the town (*gorispolkom*) and its chairman— the equivalent of town councils and mayors. It is the custom that such executives sit on the bureau of the corresponding committee of the Party, but not on its secretariat. Those who work in the Party "apparatus" do so full time and have no other occupation.

The Komsomol, a faithful replica of the Party, is also divided into *obkoms* and *kraikoms, gorkoms,* and *raikoms*, secretariats and departments. Thus Mikhail Gorbachev started his career in 1955 at the bottom, but, within a few months, he was assigned to a job "related to his juridicial education," probably somewhere in the judicial apparatus in Stavropol. His official biography is hazy about the first year: "works for the Komsomol and the Party," is the entry for 1956. Dev Murarka thinks that he was head of a department of the Komsomol *gorkom* in Stavropol, which seems very likely, although rather humble for a graduate of the Law Faculty.[1] But he did not have to go back to his village and lived instead in the regional capital—a young peasant turned into a city dweller—while still involved in agriculture although not with tractors and combine harvesters.

It is significant that Gorbachev worked simultaneously in the same year both in the Komsomol and in the Party apparatus. This means that the twenty–four–year–old official showed enough promise, and after a few months in a subaltern Komsomol job he was sent for a probationary period to work in the local Party apparatus, probably in one of the *gorkom* departments. There he gained enough experience to return to the Komsomol in a more responsible position, and as early as 1956 he was appointed first secretary of the Stavropol Komsomol *gorkom.* The *apparatchik* was now ready for the way up.

Stavropol as it is now looks quite pleasant. It stands in a plateau some 600 meters above the steppe, and if rather windswept, nestles in rich vegetation. It can boast many parks and tree–lined avenues whose names unfortunately conform to the Soviet patterns. There is the Karl Marx Street, the "Soviet" Street, the Dzerzhinski Street, and the ubiquitous Lenin Square, a large empty space where the May Day and November parades are held. In the 1950s an enormous bunker was built in the "Stalinist" style (granite up to the first floor, a marble portico, with columns going up to the roof) to house the Party territorial committee and the territorial council, as well as the *kraikom* and *kraispolkom.* The offices for the town itself, Gorkam and Gorispolkom, were a few steps away in an older building, which was the Tsarist Governor's seat before the revolution. However, it is a small city (300,000 inhabitants now, nearly one–half in 1957) occupying the 70th rank among Soviet cities. It stands isolated from the main centers of civilization, and was founded as a garrison town for the imperial army and government officials. In 1932 it had only twenty–five stone buildings, it did not have a bus service until 1928, and planes could not land there before 1935. Thus, undoubtedly, Mikhail Gorbachev has been influenced by his country background, by life in a provincial backwater where everybody knows everybody else, and outsiders are few and far between.

Vsevolod Murakhovski: His Superior and Ally from the Early Days

Quite a lot is known of an early protector of the budding states-man. Vsevolod Murakhovski was older than Gorbachev by five years and a Party member since 1946. He led the Komsomol *gorkom* in 1954. He must have been impressed with the newly arrived, Moscow-trained lawyer. He himself only had a diploma from the local Teacher Training college. He was sent to work in the Party apparatus in 1956 and recommended Gorbachev as his successor. They kept in close touch during the following years spent in various other jobs, until the younger man outran his erstwhile superior and became his protector. In 1985, Murakhovski became a member of the Central Committee, first deputy chairman of the USSR government, and head of the agro-industrial committee, for whose failure he is reported to be responsi-ble. He was sacked in 1989, showing that it is not sufficient to be a friend of the Secretary General.

Unlike Murakhovski, who only stayed two years in the Komso-mol, Gorbachev was an official of the Communist Youth Organization for almost seven years, until March 1962. He was first secretary of the Komsomol *gorkom*, that is leader of the town organization from 1956 to 1958; second secretary of the Komsomol *kraikom* (territory level), later first secretary from 1958 to 1962. It was a smooth career, if it were not for a curious interlude in 1958 which lasted for a few months. He was by then second–in–command in the department of agitation and propaganda of the Komsomol *kraikom*, a surprisingly subaltern position for a person who was soon to rise to become head man of the town of Stavropol and then second–in–command of the entire territory. Thus, he should have been number one, not a deputy of the *agitprop*. This slight career upset cannot be explained. How-ever, if one bears in mind a similar incident at Moscow University in 1954, it appears that Gorbachev's progress, although overall decid-edly steady, must have included a few reverses. It shows a resilience of character that he overcame them.

All of this should be considered in the context of contemporary events, Khrushchev's triumphant ascension entailed restructuring of the Party machine, reshuffling of personnel and changes in the leadership of the party and government. With destalinization going on old feuds were also settled. In Stavropol it was obvious that the Party organization found it difficult to adjust to the new ways, more so than in other parts of the country. In addition many fallen leaders were relegated to the area and Moscow did not cease to attack the local apparatus. Stavropol communists fought back with attempts at obstructing reforms and in 1961 helped in bringing about Khrushchev's downfall. Of course, Mikhail Gorbachev was still a minor official who could not play a significant part in the struggle, but he must have been aware of it.

Stavropol As a Garbage Dump

In April 1956, following the 20th Congress, the *kraikom's* first secretary, Ivan Boytsov, who succeeded Suslov in 1945, was removed. He was not actually demoted since he was immediately appointed deputy chairman—soon to become first deputy chairman of the Party's Central Committee in Moscow. However, it was considered no rise, and the man was by no means a follower of Khrushchev; he was retired in 1961, before the 22nd Party Congress, when he lost his seat on the Central Committee. From then on no more was heard of him. Besides, local Party history shows that at the *kraikom* meeting of April 1956, during which Boytsov was relieved of his functions, "serious shortcomings" in agriculture were revealed. The first secretary as well as the *kraikom* bureau were blamed.

Boytsov was succeeded by Ivan Lebedev, also a veteran of Stalin's apparatus (he was in charge of the Party at Penza, later Omsk), whose period of power ended even more ingloriously. On January 28, 1960, he was dismissed without being given an alternative job and died in complete oblivion in 1972. In spite of a good harvest in 1958, for which the territory won the decoration of the Order of Lenin in the same year, Khrushchev behaved very harshly toward Lebedev, whom he violently scolded at the plenary session in December 1958. It later became known, from a speech made by Dmitri Polyansky at the January 1961 plenum, that in 1959 the local Stavropol leaders "bought most of their deliveries of cows from the population and sent them to government butchers" to fulfill the plan. Since the cows were sold at a much cheaper rate than they had been bought, the operation resulted in enormous losses for the region's *kolkozes* and *sovkhozes*. Furthermore, the number of sheep had declined by 138,000 heads.[2]

Was the region getting the right first secretary? Not yet, since Lebedev's successor was also demoted, and his rule was to be even shorter. Nikolai Belyaev, when he was appointed as leader of the *krai* in January 1960, was still a full Politburo member—a post he occupied since 1957—and by then he had already fallen out of Khrushchev's favor. He had just lost a much more important position as first secretary at Kazakhstan, where he had incurred Khrushchev's wrath because of poor management of the virgin lands. He might have been used as a scapegoat after the violent riots that occurred at Temir Tau, an industrial area in the republic in September 1959, which resulted in numerous deaths. Leonid Brezhnev went to Alma-Ata to supervise his dismissal and replace him with an unknown local leader, Kunaev. In Belyaev's case, Stavropol was the last stage of his final downfall. On June 25, 1960, barely five months later, the *kraikom* chose Fedor Kulakov as first secretary. This was the end of Belyaev who was retired at the age of fifty-seven and died unnoticed in October 1966.

Bulganin's Punishment

Finally Fedor Kulakov was to be the "real" chief. Before describing this important party figure, a few words should be said about the fate of Nikolai Bulganin after he was sent to Stavropol, illustrating the fact that it was a kind of limbo for many of the *nomenklatura* (party appointed senior officials). Though the latter was not as well known as Molotov, Malenkov or Zhukov, he was a celebrity of Stalin's regime; he was a marshal, twice defense minister, a Politburo member since 1948, chairman of the Council of Ministers from 1955 to 1958, Khrushchev's second-in-command (the famous tandem) at the Geneva summit in 1955 and on international visits throughout the world. Bulganin unfortunately made the mistake of supporting the "Molotov faction" in its attempt to topple Khrushchev from power. As the latter commented: "Bulganin reached for the gingerbread offered to him by the anti-party group."[3]

At the time nothing was known of Bulganin's blunder. The Central Committee merely inflicted on him a "serious admonition" in return for self-criticism, but in secret. In the following year, Khrushchev launched the final assault on his old opponent and dismissed him from his position as Prime Minister on March 27, 1958. The party chief replaced him and assumed both functions. Later still, on September 5, Bulganin lost his seat in the Politburo. In November Khrushchev came out in the open against Bulganin, who in December was forced to humiliate himself in a "confession" at another plenum. (The Central Committee met six times in Moscow in 1958, three more than usual.)

On March 31, Bulganin was appointed director of the USSR National Bank, but in view of the renewed backbiting, he had to be moved away from Moscow. Four months later, while still a member of the Politburo, he was sent into exile at Stavropol as chairman of the regional council for national economy, one of the *sovharkhozes* created by Khrushchev in the past year, to try and decentralize the management of industry. It was expected that he would retain his position only for a few months, to save face, before being retired for good. It turned out that Bulganin remained in office until 1960, in spite of furious attacks against him during 1958 and 1959 when he reached the legal age of retirement. He was not excluded from the central committee either, and kept his seat up to the 1961 Congress. He died in Moscow in February 1975.

Stavropol had to suffer the consequences. First of all, the local elite felt both curiousity and embarrassment about the presence of the prestigious "has been," just as it would later about another ex-Politburo member, Belyaev. Second, it was damaging for the *krai* to be considered as "another Mongolia," a remote province for fallen party celebrities (the first mission given to Molotov after his downfall was that of Ambassador to Mongolia). Finally, exile in Stavropol was not enough to save the poor wretches from Khrushchev's ire. (For example, violent criticism of the Stavropol *sovnarkhoze* appeared in *Pravda* on December 12, 1958). These public attacks also damaged local establishments and cast a shadow on other people's careers.

What did Mikhail Gorbachev think of these developments? The Komsomol leader must have run across Bulganin and Bolyaev often during those years, but neither his functions nor his rank called for close relations with them. It must have given him first-hand experience both of the precarious nature of a political career and the need for choosing his allies advisedly. Soon the future Party Secretary General was able to find a sponsor to help him on his ascent to power.

Fedor Kulakov in the Role of a Godfather

When he took on the job of First Secretary of the Stavropol *kraikom* in June 1960, Fedor Kulakov was manifestly destined to last longer than his predecessors. Although he also came from Moscow he was not in disgrace. In the capital he was neither a Politburo member nor chairman of the Council of Ministers, but only a deputy minister of Agriculture of the Russian Federation (since 1955), and later minister for cereals and bread consumption in the same republic (since 1959). In other words, he managed to make his way through the various upheavals caused by Khrushchev in agriculture, and his coming to Stavropol was undoubtedly an advancement; a year later, in 1961, he was in fact given full membership in the Central Committee. He was only forty-two years old in 1961 and, like Gorbachev, was of peasant extraction; according to rumors in Stavropol, he was of Cossack descent. (Cossacks were peasants who had been freed from serfdom, half-farmers, half-soldiers, renowned for their fierce independence). A significant factor in his career was that he started in the Penza region, in the center of European Russia, where he worked between 1945 and 1948 under Konstantin Chernenko. It is true that he was not particularly well educated, but his diploma from the Federal Agricultural Institute, which he passed in 1957 after preparing for it by correspondence, gave him more credibility in agriculture than any of his predecessors.

Henceforth, Kulakov played a decisive part in the career of the young Komsomol territorial leader, though they had never before met. He was the one who guided Mikhail Gorbachev in 1962, when he left the Komsomol to take over two important posts. First, in March, in the wake of another Khrushchev attempt at agricultural redeployment, there was an urgent need for managers in the "territorial production units for *kolkhozes* and *sovkhozes*," which replaced the traditional boroughs (*raion*) and were an early form of the "agro-industrial cooperatives" established twenty years later. Sixteen such units were constituted in the Stavropol territory (for twenty-one boroughs) and Gorbachev became Party organizer in one of them. This appointment is seen by commentators as a decline, but it does not seem to be so in Gorbachev's case. Normally a Komsomol leader was given the appointment as first secretary of a *raikom* (borough), but since he was put in charge of a more important body, he was advancing faster.

However, in December of that year Gorbachev's luck turned. The territorial production units were found unsatisfactory, so Khrushchev decided on a more drastic overhaul of agriculture. Later he was violently attacked for these changes which disappeared with him. The Party apparatus was divided into two: one for industry and the other for agriculture. Two *kraikoms* were created in Stavropol; the more important in this essentially rural region was the agricultural *kraikom*, which was given to the second secretary of the old *kraikom*, Nikolai Bosenko.

Mikhail Gorbachev became chief of the department of Party organization for the *kraikom*. It is not clear whether this was the agricultural *kraikom*, but it is likely in view of his future relationship with Kulakov. In other words, at the age of thirty–one, Gorbachev was in charge of the most important command in the regional party apparatus where he controlled appointments of local *nomenklatura* members. It is obvious that this promotion was approved by the central authorities in Moscow, but Kulakov's recommendation was a key factor. Gorbachev remained in the department for almost four years, to September 1966.

This coincided with Khrushchev's fall and Brezhnev's rise to power. It is interesting to see the reactions of the Stavropol region's elite to this shift of influence. There is little doubt that relations between Khrushchev and Kulakov, the local potentate, had been strained. An important plenum was held in January 1961 on agriculture. Not only did Kulakov remain silent, but only he among the first secretaries of the main agricultural regions was not a member of the commission which drafted the resolution. The person who reported on Stavropol was Dmitry Polyansky, a Politburo member, who gave a sorry account of misappropriation of funds in 1959. The blame fell on Lebedev, who had already been dismissed, but *Pravda* renewed its attack a few days later and chose *kraikom* officials who were still in office as a target. "They still follow the beaten track of recommendations from above, without taking local circumstances into account and without discussing the problems with agricultural workers."[4] The territory was also criticized for mismanagement of agriculture in *Soviet Russia* on May 23, 1962.

Judged a competent leader of men, Kulakov was spared criticism. In July 1961, Khrushchev's visit to the territory went smoothly. He gave a dispassionate account of the discussions on the spot in a note submitted to the Politburo (presidium at the time). He even regarded Manyakin highly (he was then chairman of the *kraispolkom*, in other words the territorial government leader.[5] Not long afterwards Manyakin was appointed inspector of the Central Committee, followed later by an appointment as first secretary of the Omsk (*omkom*), where he remained until 1987.

On the other hand, Kulakov was not overjoyed to have his territory turned into a testing ground for the mercurial Nikita's uncoordinated ventures. More significantly, he seems to have resented Khrushchev's drive against Stalin and the anti–Party faction. This became obvious at the 22nd Party Congress, which was held in October 1961 in Moscow. The occasion marked the first appearance of Mikhail Gorbachev at an event of national importance in the Kremlin.

The 22nd Congress

Gorbachev, at the age of thirty and a local Komsomol leader, was chosen as delegate to the Congress. Together with a few scores of local *nomenklatura* members and elite workers he was included in the Stavropol "delegation," which entitled him to take part in the election of the new Central Committee. Evidently this was all he was allowed to do, for it was out of the question that he should be elected to the Central Committee—this came ten years later—or even that he should address the assembly, a privilege granted only to much more important figures.

In addition, Gorbachev was allowed to attend the Congress thanks to an increase in delegates' numbers. Until that time congresses were held in the Supreme Soviet Hall, which was of modest proportions. During the summer of 1961, a new building, the impressive "Palace of Congresses,"located at the center of the Kremlin, was completed. It was much more modern and spacious and became the subject of muted criticism on the part of guardians of the Kremlin architectural heritage. This meant that the number of delegates increased from about 1,400 at the 21st Congress, held in 1959, to 6,000. On the list of the new delegates were first secretaries of a borough (*raikom*) and regional Komsomol leaders from Saratov and Krasnodar, from Novosibirsk and Sverdlovsk, etc. Still, it was a distinction for Gorbachev to be singled out for the Congress as a Komsomol leader of a middle–sized region. He owed the favor mostly to the head of the delegation, Fedor Kulakov.

At the Congress two signs indicated that the leader and his team were not in sympathy with the new political line. From the start the Congress turned into an orgy of denunciations of the "personality cult" and of its chief priests within (the anti–party faction) and without. Albania was criticized openly, together with Mao Tse Tung's China. The Congress' final resolution ordered the removal of Stalin's embalmed body from the mausoleum where it lay beside Lenin. Voroshilov, the last member of the "anti–party" still in power, had also been accused and "confessed" to political errors, while new revelations were made regarding Molotov, Malenkov, and Kaganovich, not to mention Bulganin and his political errors.

In fact an analysis of the speeches delivered by the various leaders shows a marked difference in opinion. Some denounced the "crimes" of the fallen men, demanding their expulsion from the Party as well as their trials by tribunals. Others evoked mistakes not involving legal action. A third group emphasized the fact that the Party revealed the "whole truth" about the dark events of the 1930s, and that it was time to leave things alone and stop witch hunts which might lead to purges. This "soft" group won in the end, since Molotov was not expelled from the Party until three years later in 1961. (He was reinstated by Chernenko twenty years later.) Moreover, the idea of a monument to Stalin's victims, which was put forward by Khrushehev, was quietly buried.

The Silence of the Stavropol Contingent

Another group of participants preferred to keep quiet. Kulakov and his Stavropol party belonged to this group. About 200 speakers took the floor, including over a hundred discounted spokesmen from the "fraternal parties." The list of speakers was open, since Khrushchev needed support to overcome some reluctance by the Politburo. Kulakov, who alone was entitled to speak, preferred to keep silent, and probably not without reason. He let Dmitry Polyansky, another speaker, denounce the "mass repressions of the Kuban," for which Kaganovich was blamed.

The Moscow authorities could not fail to view this attitude with displeasure, and it became apparent a few weeks after the Congress in December 1961. Then a resolution was approved by the Central Committee Bureau for the Russian Republic (RSFSR), with Khrushchev presiding, denouncing "grave shortcomings in elucidation and a request to study the documents prepared for the 22nd Congress in the Stavropol territory." This declaration was printed in a periodical entitled *Party Life* in February 1962, but a fuller analysis of it is available in the local Party history:

> The resolution pointed out that propagation of the Congress documents was often carried out in the territory in an abstract way, not always answering the needs of the present. . . . The necessary conclusions were drawn. At its January 1962 meeting, the *kraikom* plenum decided what was to be

done in concrete terms, in what way and in what space of
time, to remedy the shortcomings. The plenum demanded
that the *kraikom* bureau . . . tighten its control over the
ideological content of propaganda and agitation.[6]

In plain language this meant that Kulakov, maybe imitating
Suslov whom he succeeded at Stavrpol and whose position later became clearer, did not agree with Khrushchev's policy of washing dirty
linen in public since they were both afraid it might destabilize the
system. He may also have thought that anti–Stalin campaigns would
come to an end soon and that it was prudent to wait and see. Suslov
influenced his friends and subordinates in this sense, which explains
why the Stavropol Party kept silent during the Congress and why the
local apparatus did not show much vigor in informing "the masses
of the conclusions reached by the Congress." Reprisals ensued in
the form of the above–mentioned resolution. Kulakov pretended to
comply, but little changed in real terms.

Mikhail Gorbachev was among Kulakov's subordinates whose
task was, as a delegate to the Congress, to spread the word to outly-
ing villages. What were his real feelings toward Khrushchev and his
upheavals? The direction he took after 1986 shows that deep down
he must have approved of this early form of "restructuring." Did he
not pay homage on November 1, 1987 to the "courageous" initiatives
taken by Khrushchev? But for the time being it was better for him
to tow the Kulakov line. He still conformed to such views in 1967,
and he expounded them in banal and rigorously orthodox terms to
Mlynar when they met:

Gorbachev was not sorry for Khrushchev's disappearance.
He thought his unceasing interference in the economy, especially in agriculture, was rather harmful, because it was
usually done on an impulse and often for purely subjective
reasons. His main objection to Khrushchev was that he still
followed the old fashioned way of arbitrary centralism.[7]

What Gorbachev fails to reveal is the part that Kulakov, his boss,
played in the palace revolution which brought Khrushchev down in
October 1964. According to the Medvedev brothers, a meeting held
on the banks of Lake Manych in the Stavropol area had sparked off the
plot one month earlier, on the occasion of a protracted shooting ex-
pedition which brought together several Politburo members—among
them Suslov—and their host Fedor Kulakov.[8] This may be possible,

but it seems rather surprising that people involved in the plot were not afraid to have a mere Central Committee member attend such crucial discussions while other Politburo members were kept in the dark.

On the other hand, what is certain is that Kulakov was one of the first beneficiaries of the changes in Moscow. Only two people were sacked in November 1964 at the same time as Khrushchev: Adzhubey, his embarrassing son–in–law, and Vasily Polyakov, the most recent of his assistants in agriculture, secretary, and head of the agriculture department of the Central Committee since 1962. There was no need to replace the son–in–law in a party office, except on the editorial board of *Izvestia*, where he was during Khrushchev's years in power. But Polyakov needed a successor and Kulakov was chosen. In December 1964, he went to Moscow where he became head of the agriculture department. Starting in September 1965 he combined that job with that of secretary, thereby ensuring him a meteoric rise.

The Stavropol team, including Gorbachev, was left without a leader. For the first time in postwar years since Suslov held the office its leader was not shamefully sacked on the spot. On the contrary, he was sent to Moscow where he could act as a powerful protector for the region. To start with it looked as if Stavropol would still be used as a place of exile for government members in disgrace. Kulakov's successor was a Politburo candidate member, Leonid Efremov, who had been previously first deputy chairman of the Central Committee bureau for the Russian republic—a much more exalted position— making him number two in the Russian party, the most important republic in the Union. The old *apparatchik*, who had been first secretary of the prestigious Gorky region, found himself downgraded when sent to Stavropol, due to Kirilenko's growing influence. The latter was Efremov's partner at the head of the bureau for the Russian Republic. But Khrushchev's downfall put him in third position in the USSR, after Brezhnev and Suslov.

This time the transition was much easier. First of all, the "punishment" meted out was painless—Efremov stayed in the Politburo as a full member for eighteen months. Only at the 1966 Congress was he not re–elected. Second, he had a reputation for being a courteous and civilized person (*"kulturny"* is the adjective still used in Stavropol), and he got along easily with local leaders. He preferred to keep the "Kulakov team" unchanged and Mikhail Gorbachev retained his position as chief of the cadre department. In fact, under Efremov's rule, the future Secretary General enjoyed rapid advancement as a regional *apparatchik*. He was made first secretary of Stavropol *gorkom* (city) in September 1966, second secretary of *kraikom* (territory) in August 1968, and first secretary of the *kraikom*, in place of Efremov, in June 1970.

It is significant that at the time Gorbachev's two immediate superiors continued to enjoy his favors after he assumed power in 1985. In 1986 Efremov was reelected as member of the Central Revision Commission (the third rank of the *nomenklatura*, just below full member and candidate of the Central Committee), and retained that post until he was seventy-eight years old, and in spite of the new fashion for younger cadres, he is first deputy chairman of the government committee for science and technology. His other superior was Ivan Kapitonov, who has been head of the cadre department in Moscow since 1965, at the time Gorbachev was in charge of the same for the territory. In 1986, at the age of seventy-two, Kapitonov was still chairman of the Central Revision Commission.

Thus, everything seemed promising for Gorbachev early in the Brezhnev era. At the age of thirty-five he already occupied a fairly powerful position with a great deal of potential (*perspektivny* is the Russian word). His chiefs were well-disposed toward him, and he was the protégé of a rising figure in the capital. Though his education was better than that of the average local *apparatchik*, since he was a graduate of the University of Moscow, he was eager to learn more about agriculture, the main economic activity of the region. From 1963 or 1964 through 1966, he enrolled in a correspondence course with the Stavropol Agricultural Institute. Needless to say, he passed his exams with flying colors, for one could not possibly fail the first *gorkom* secretary, the most influential man in town! This academic activity coincided with Raisa's research in the local *kolkhozes* and the defense of her thesis in Moscow.

The Gorbachevs' Travel Abroad: 5,500 Kms through France

The couple was enjoying all the usual privileges bestowed by the Soviet regime on its dignitaries. They were even greater than before for Brezhnev's years in power were heralded as the golden age for the *nomenklatura*. A privilege unknown in Stalin's days was the possibility of travelling abroad. When Gorbachev was given national responsibilities he naturally went on countless foreign trips but, already in his Stavropol days before 1978, he had travelled abroad several times.

Curiously enough, at this stage he went to Western developed countries, traveling three times to France in 1966, 1975, and 1976, Belgium in 1972, West Germany in 1975, and Czechoslovakia in 1967.

This is not an exhaustive list, for there is no complete record in the West of the innumerable delegations that Moscow sent abroad in the years of detente, and some still being discovered to this day. Thus, for example, it was thought that Gorbachev had visited Italy in 1981, on the occasion of the funeral of the communist leader Berliguer. Subsequently he revealed in an interview to *Unita* in May 1987 that he already knew the country, having toured Sicily and visiting Turin and Florence at an unspecified date.[9] Since at the time he was a member of a delegation of "party officials," it is probable that the visit took place while he was still in the province.

This being the case, there is no doubt that his first forays into the outside world must have counted among the most rewarding. Two separate trips are worth examining in detail: his first visit to France in 1966 and his journey to Czechoslovakia three years later.

As for his trip to France, it is neither confirmed nor denied by the French Communist Party, which when asked to consult their archives discovered only two instances of Gorbachev staying at their invitation in those years: one was on "holidays" in 1975, and the other was with a delegation of farming experts in 1976. The 1966 trip, however, was personally confirmed by Gorbachev in October 1985 when he made an official visit to Paris. Looking back with pleasure upon this episode, the Secretary General answered our question: "Yes, and we drove for 5,500 kms through France in a Renault." In all likelihood this stay took place at the invitation of Jean–Baptiste Doumeng, the well–known "Red Millionaire," who is now deceased. He was a tycoon in the agro–industrial field and traded with the Soviet Union. He regularly inviting Soviet farming personalities to France. Doumeng did confirm that he entertained Mikhail Gorbachev and knew him well. At the age of thirty–five, when Gorbachev still occupied a fairly humble position in the Party hierachy (in the summer of 1966 he was head of the Party Organization department for the Stavropol territory), he toured France, and in particular the southwest (Doumeng's territory) without the constraints of a "red carpet" and the protocol that he was to experience later on. This must have been a useful glimpse of the way capitalist country workers made a living within the time frame of their living conditions compared with those of the "socialist paradise."

Another discovery was made on his trip to Czechoslovakia. It was a country close to his heart, since the first foreigner who became his friend was the Czech student Zdenek Mlynar. This was all the more so a few months after Soviet troops had invaded and occupied Prague in August 1968, an event that had caused a stir in the USSR and had shaken the international communist movement. It should be remembered that the political situation was far from "normalized" in Czechoslovakia in 1969. Dubcek gave up power only in April of that year, and the people enjoyed the freedom of the Prague Spring for at least two more years. At the same time, in an attempt to accelerate normalization and to renew in a rather pathetic way the "special Soviet–Czechosolvak relationship," Moscow was sending one delegation after another to Prague. For that reason Gorbachev, who was second secretary of the Stavropol territory, was included in a party of "young Party officials who [had] previously worked in the Komsomol, the youth movement."

This time we know a little more of his reactions from observations he made during a "walkabout" on a journey to Czechoslovakia he made in April 1987. He admitted that the stiuation had been grim:

There were seventeen youth organizations in Czechoslovakia in those days—a hodge–podge resembling the confused ideas of most young people. I remember though that the young were trying to understand the real truth. This was a difficult time, but it gave rise to anguished reflection and a great deal of heart searching. I am glad that we were standing next to you in those trying days.[10]

Two days later, in Bratislava, he touched on the same subject:

My first stay here took place in a period which was far from easy. We were with you in those difficult days, when you were trying to preserve honor and dignity. We reflected courageously on the events and learned the hard way . .
   drawing the right conclusions. You know full well that Czechoslovakia made great strides in the years following 1968.[11]

It is interesting to see that the *apparatchik* and future Kremlin autocrat felt scornful about the multiplicity of Czech youth organizations, which he called a "hodge–podge." He said nothing about the intervention itself. However, he did not refer specifically to this event and refrained from using the term "counterrevolution," a term dear to Husak when attacking Dubcek and his team and the Prague Spring. He seems to imply that both sides were to blame. In November 1987, two years before the revolutions in Eastern Europe, the head of the Soviet Institute of Marxism–Leninism went so far as to say that a "fresh look" at the 1968 events in Czechoslovakia was necessary. What could be more natural than to make use of the affair to illustrate the dangers implicit in a rejection of *perestroika*.

1970: The "Prefect" of Stavropol

One year after the trip to Czechoslovakia, on June 17, 1970, Mikhail Gorbachev became first secretary of the *kraikom*, that is to say the most influential person in the Stavropol territory. The role played by first regional secretaries in the USSR has rightly been compared by the American expert Jerry Hough to that of *préfets* in France. At a regional level he represented the central power—the Party in this case—and enjoyed all the authority, prestige, and privileges which go with the function in a highly centralized totalitarian system. As a political leader he is also required to find raw materials or spare parts for factories, to fix the day for sowing and harvesting, and to conduct these operations like a general leading his troops into battle while shouting rallying cries, encouragements, and sending triumphant "reports" to the center. He is a man who holds all the strings of the economy, culture, and communication, one whose power has no limits except those set by orders and emissaries from Moscow.

Naturally the position is not without danger. If something goes wrong, especially if the region fails to fulfill the Plan, the first secretary is made a scapegoat. Still, as Brezhnev's motto was complete confidence, even blind faith, in the cadres, the dangers were smaller than at any other time in Soviet history. Two–thirds of the first regional secretaries in power in July 1970 were still occupying the same functions five years later, while half of them remained until 1980. It should also be remembered that Mikhail Gorbachev enjoyed the patronage of Kulakov in Moscow itself.

In the Soviet apparatus other offices go with the principal job. Gorbachev assumed them in quick succession. In June 1970 he was elected deputy to the Supreme Soviet of the USSR in the central Stavropol constituency, which comprised the Krasnogvardeiskoe and the village where he was born, Privolnoe. In April of the following year, the 24th Congress made him a full member of the Central

Committee, without the intermediate period of candidate member-
ship. Another notable result of this "successful" congress was that
Fedor Kulakov entered the Politburo. Since he kept his post in the
Secretariat, he became a "super secretary" (both full member of the
Politburo and secretary), member of the inner circle from which a
secretary general is chosen.

A Young Man in the Geriatocracy

Kulakov became one of the youngest members of the Politburo
(together with Shelepin and Shcherbitsky, also born in 1918), but soon
they were overtaken by their fellow Stavropol member Gorbachev.
His appointment as first *kraikom* secretary had already made him the
youngest such official in the Soviet Union. Only two other men born
in the thirties, Vasily Demidenko in North Kazahstan and Alexander Gudkov at Kursk, were about his age. Likewise in the Central
Committee, the forty–odd–year old Gorbachev was outdone as full
member only by Valentina Nikolaeva–Tereshkova, the female cosmo-
naut who was born in 1937, and by a few elite workers. No *apparatchik*
could compare in age to him, and in fact he was seen more and more
as the odd man out in a team of decrepit old men. It was not surprising under these circumstances that he was made chairman of the
Commission for Youth in the Supreme Soviet.

It should not be assumed that the youthful regional leader stood
out among the others for his modern look. In a photograph taken in
1970 when he was on a walk around Stavropol, Gorbachev appears
totally different, but not younger. He was much heavier than he is
now and he was already balding, dressed in an ill–fitting suit made of
coarse fabric, giving the appearance of a typical country *apparatchik*.
His national responsibilities led him to lose weight and improve his
general appearance.

It should not be assumed either that Mikhail Gorbachev was
keen to promote people of his own generation. He was obviously not
the only person in charge of career advancement in Stavropol, but he
consistently showed a tendency to choose considerably older people
to work with. Several members of "Misha's gang," as they would be
called in another environment, became well known later. Besides the
faithful Murakhovsky, who took over from his erstwhile subordinate
as chairman of the Stavropol *gorkom* before becoming head of the
Karachays autonomous region, there was Vladimir Kalashnikov, an
agronomist who moved up three times under Gorbachev's rule in the

region (chief of the water department, then head of the agriculture department on the Party Committee, and later *kraikom* secretary); he is now the regional secretary of the important Volgograd area. His deputy Alexander Budyka is now minister for cereals and bread consumption. Boris Volodin, another agronomist and *kolkhoz* chairman in the fifties and sixties and also chief of the agriculture department in the Stavropol *kraikom* under Gorbachev, has been first secretary of the neighboring area of Rostov since January 1986. Veniamin Afonin, first borough (*raikom*) secretary in the territory throughout the Gorbachev era, was moved up to head of the Chemical Industry department of the Central Committee in February 1983. Others failed to rise, as the *kraikom* secretary Ivan Taranov, who was appointed chairman of the regional council (*kraispolkom*) in 1973 and is still in the same position.

Gorbachev remained the top man in Stavropol for eight years. In the soporific climate of the Brezhnev era and its secretiveness, little is known of his activities. Few details from provincial life find an echo in the capital, apart from occasional reports of success in fulfilling the Plan and routine criticisms. As is the case for those regions whose main activity lies in agriculture, everything revolves around harvesting, government deliveries, and sowing "campaigns," which by universal consent could not be launched without Party control and encouragement from the Agitprop.

Since Stavropol is an area of comparative prosperity, Gorbachev's task was easier than in the days when he would be put in charge of agriculture for the entire country. For a time his harvests proved satisfactory and he even enjoyed a bumper crop in 1976. A rather obscure episode shows his difficulty in getting used to political, technocratic niceties which are the bread and butter of an *apparatchik* in the USSR.

The Ipatovo Experiment: Opportunism is Sometimes Necessary

Early in the 1970s Gorbachev introduced the system of brigades working under contract in farming; this involved small teams of a few *kolkhoz* workers together with members of their families who were paid in proportion to their yields. In 1976, he extended the system over the entire territory since it had proved successful in the chosen district in order to gently decentralize *kolkhoz* management.

In 1977, however, there was a sudden reversal in this policy. Harvesting was to be carried out by much larger teams of at least fifteen strong combine harvesters which would be moved with all their equipment and numerous attendants from one unit to the other. An experiment was carried out in the Ipatov borough, located near Gorbachev's home village, which gave its name to the experiment, thereby receiving national fame. In 1977 crops were stored up in a record nine days. A triumphant report was sent to "Comrade Brezhnev," who duly sent his congratulations by telegram. With unusual speed *Pravda* published on July 16 a special decree of the Central Committee to the effect that "the Ipatovo *raikom*'s experiment in garnering crops" would be applied everywhere.

Of course the youthful first *kraikom* secretary took credit for this "success," giving an interview on the very same day to journalists of the Party daily and publishing many articles on the subject in the national press. At the 1979 Supreme Soviet elections, Gorbachev had his constituency's boundaries redrawn, so that the celebrated Ipatovo borough was included in it.

That's when the policy was changed. Starting in 1980 all press reference to the "Ipatovo experiment" terminated in the press, Gorbachev hardly ever mentioned it in his articles and speeches, or if he did so, very briefly and in muted terms. It took several years to learn the full truth about it. On September 29, 1983, *Izvestia* made fun of these "armadas" of agricultural machinery which harvested fields at their convenience while neglecting others. It is now usually conceded that this technique of wheat production was successful only in some areas, but should not have been extended to the entire territory.

In reality, Gorbachev's policies since 1985 all point to decentralization, so it can be assumed that the Ipatovo experiment was not his brainchild. Undoubtedly it was Fedor Kulakov, who was in charge of agriculture in the Politburo at the time, who launched it in 1977. Kulakov died the following year and his invention was no longer used, so that Gorbachev could return to his own experiment, the system of brigades. Until then it was out of the question that he should distance himself from his powerful protector. Hence a lesson in opportunism which should be remembered since it throws some light on the man's character: he knows where he is going, but he can also bide his time.

There were other instances to show that problems and "experiments" which applied only to agriculture played a subsidiary part in the Secretary General's career, although his diploma in agronomy, his family background, and his years in Stavropol all made him an expert in this branch. There were also more important things to pursue, such as high politics, jockeying for power at the top, long–term planning in "positioning" oneself, as well as displaying or not displaying an attitude of cooperation toward those in power.

In public Gorbachev kept a low profile. It is significant that he did not take the platform during Party congresses in 1971, 1976 or in 1981 when he was already a Politburo member. (He remained content with chairing a session.) Kulakov had chosen the same tactic at the 1961 Congress, but this was probably due to a difference in outlook. The same explanation could not be applied to the congresses of the Brezhnev era since they were uneventful and conformed to the established rules of protocol. In addition the Stavropol territory, considered comparatively of minor importance, did not entitle its representative to address congresses as a matter of course. For this reason Gorbachev remained silent while his more prominent neighbors, Medunov (Krasnodar) or Bondarenko (Rostov) were regular speakers.

Brezhnev and the Spas

Gorbachev was not adverse to sacrificing to the idol of the day— Brezhnev. A thorough search through the local archives can yield its quota of relevant information. Here is a jewel in the form of a speech delivered by Gorbachev in May 1978 during an ideological conference in Stavropol. Due to its geographical location, the Stavropol officials had to join in the strident campaign of adulation that had been conducted for many years around the so–called "Little Land" battle, a war battle which had taken place near their territory and which had been blown out of proportion because Brezhnev had been involved in it. It became something resembling Stalingrad in importance. The first *kraikom* secretary was pleased to announce that "because of the countless requests from the Stavropol workers," the two local newspapers published a book written by Brezhnev in installments. He went on to say:

> The book entitled *The Little Land*, although a short work, shines by its ideological contents and the breadth of the commentaries and judgments expressed by its author, so that it has become a great event in public life. It has found a warm welcome in Soviet hearts. . . . Communists and all workers of Stavropol express their most heartfelt thanks

to Leonid Illyich Brezhnev for this literary and Party work which describes with great philosophical depth the courses of the heroic deed of our beloved country, its moral and spiritual strength, its tenacity and courage.[12]

It should be noted that this laudatory passage was written a few months before Mikhail Gorbachev was appointed as party secretary in Moscow. With hindsight it appears as a vital element of his crossing the boundary between provincial and national leadership. Another way of making one's way in Soviet politics was to take care of the tourists that visited the Stavropol territory, in particular the many *nomenklatura* members who came to take the waters.

The Kislovodsk and Piatigorsk waters are beneficial for kidney ailments. Yuri Andropov returned to his homeland for treatment, as did Suslov, Kosygin, and Kirilenko. Brezhnev came less frequently since he preferred Sochi where his devoted Medunov was the top leader, or the Crimea. Other less exalted figures were also well received by Gorbachev. He made it his duty to greet his colleagues and superiors in person, to supervise their accommodations and see to their recreation, thereby cultivating useful contacts.

The future Secretary General did not try to conceal these useful connections. In an interview he gave in May 1985 to the Moscow correspondent of Press Trust of India he answered a question regarding Suslov and Andropov in this way. *Pravda* deleted part of the interview, but Dev Muraka, an Indian, obtained the document:

> I met both leaders, Suslov and Andropov, when I worked for the Party, especially after I became chief of the Party regional organization in Stavropol and member of the Central Committee in 1971. From that time, in view of my new responsibilities, I had access to several leaders—Leonid Brezhnev, Mikhail Suslov, Yuri Andropov, and others. I do not think this is an exhaustive list. Naturally I gained political experience from these encounters. Each of them could share something with me. This is nothing unusual.[13]

This may be the case, but to a trained eye it stands out that Suslov and Andropov were selected for special treatment during their Stavropol stays. Brezhnev figured low on the list at the time of "fresh responsibilities" which started in 1978 when Gorbachev "went to Moscow."

Chapter IV

THE PRETENDER (1978–1985)

On November 27, 1978 Mikhail Gorbachev was appointed secretary of the Central Committee of the Soviet CP at the age of forty-seven. This was a major step in his career, once again breaking all records, since he was four years younger than Yakov Ryabov, another younger secretary (currently Ambassador in Paris), and more significantly eighteen years younger than the eleven secretaries.

The newly elected secretary hastily made his farewells in Stavropol passing on his powers to Vselovod Murakhovsky, a man whom he could trust implicitly. As he had done so in 1950, he made his way up to Moscow, although in a very different fashion for it was not the old university and overcrowded student hostels that awaited him. Instead he and his wife moved into a new five–room apartment located near the center of the city in Alexei Tolstoy Street; they were not the prestigious apartments on Granovski Street or Kutozov Avenue which housed the Politburo members, where Gorbachev moved in 1981. Soon thereafter his daughter Irini married a doctor and gave birth to a little girl, Oksana. The youngest member of the supreme leadership and a recent grandfather, Mikhail Gorbachev was an eminently attractive figure. Fate seemed to smile upon him.

Fedor Kulakov's Death

As miracles do not occur in isolation, it is necessary to look at Gorbachev's recent past to understand why he ended up in Moscow. A major event had occurred four months earlier, on July 17, 1978, when Fedor Kulakov suddenly died. "His heart stopped beating" was the communiqué issued by Professor Chazov, one of the most eminent members of Soviet medicine who is currently the Health Minister.

Even at that time the simple explanation appeared somewhat suspicious for the youngest member of the Politburo (after Romanov), apparently in good health, to die suddenly. Additional questions were raised at the time of his funeral when it became apparent that neither Brezhnev, Suslov, Kosygin nor Chernenko, the "junior" secretary, would attend the funeral services. Stavropol was, however, represented by Gorbachev who took the opportunity to deliver his first address from the top of Lenin's mausoleum at Red Square.

It is clear that Kulakov was one of the earliest and most significant protectors of Gorbachev. In the 1960s he showed great independence in the face of Khrushchev's whims and ideological turnabouts. This was the reason for his appointment to the leadership as Secretary of Agriculture and as full Politburo member soon after the October 1964 coup. Until his death Kulakov remained one of the four "super secretaries," preceded by Brezhnev, Kirilenko, and Suslov. Since he was twelve years younger than the youngest of the three old men it would have appeared that he was their most likely successor.

Brezhnev, whose health was fast declining (his first eclipse from public life had lasted from December 1974 to February 1975, giving rise to speculation) had to prepare his succession in earnest. According to the French President Valéry Giscard d'Estaing, Brezhnev had twice mentioned to him that he had chosen his successor. In 1975 he mentioned the Leningrad Party leader Grigory Romanov. This decision is otherwise unconfirmed except by the fact that Romanov, without having been a CC secretary, was promoted to candidate member of the Politburo in April 1973 followed by full membership in March 1976. When Brezhnev made his second choice in 1979 he allegedly declared: "Things have changed, it will now be Chernenko."

It is significant that in 1975 Brezhnev had not mentioned Kulakov, which is hardly surprising. The Stavropol figure was by no means a member of the "Brezhnev group," which had become increasingly influential during the 1970s. Members originated either from the Ukraine—in particular from Dnepropetrovsk the birthplace of the General Secretary—or from Moldavia and Kazakhstan, two republics which were under Brezhnev's control in the 1950s. Kulakov had nothing to do with these regions and his appointment was probably due to Suslov's backing. The Kremlin kingmaker had been First Secretary in Stavropol during the war and was in the habit of staying there frequently. His primary concern under Brezhnev, as well as Khrushchev, was to make sure that the leader of the day did not become too powerful and that all key positions were not in the hands of his loyal servants—in short, that a balance was kept between the various factions and groups.

The "Anti–Chernenko Candidate"

Hence one can only presume that Kulakov was the man appointed by Suslov to oppose in due course the candidate chosen by Brezhnev as his successor, Konstantin Chernenko. It is common knowledge that the latter was a spineless bureaucrat despised by the majority of Moscow *apparatchiki*, above all by those in the highest positions who did not belong to Brezhnev's camp. This can be confirmed in a comment made by Arkadi Shevchenko, Gromyko's ex–confidant, who defected to the West:

> When they were both young, Brezhnev and he [Chernenko] used to get drunk together—a custom frowned upon by the abstemious members of the political leadership, such as Suslov, Kosygin, and especially Gromyko. . . . Various key figures, Mikhail Suslov and Alexei Kosygin in particular, looked at Chernenko as an upstart, who did not have the necessary qualifications to be among them, let alone become supreme leader. . . . Though a secretary–member of the Politburo, he was considered a mere administrator, and by no means an equal.[1]

It was no accident that Kulakov was made to occupy the center stage in 1971. Among the four new full Politburo members elected at that year's congress, marking the high tide of Brezhnev's influence, three were subservient to the Secretary General or close allies: Shcherbitsky, Gishin and Kunaev. Only one, Kulakov, was independent, making up the "Suslov" counterbalance to the vast increase in Brezhnev's influence.

Once he became a member of the Politburo Kulakov managed to strengthen his own position, especially in 1976 when Dmitry Polyansky, who was known for his opposition to the Stavropol group, was evicted. Polyansky was in charge of agriculture in the Union government and Kulakov increased his powers after his downfall. However, Chernenko emerged soon as his main contender, with Brezhnev's full backing. Chernenko had been Brezhnev's right hand in Moldavia, later in the Presidium of the Supreme Soviet, of which Brezhnev was President from 1960 to 1963, and in 1965 Chernenko became head of

the "general department" of the Central Committee through which
pass all the most secret documents of the Central Committee and the
Politburo, a function which is invariably entrusted to the closest collaborator of the master of the day. In 1976 he combined the job with
that of Party Secretary. Brezhnev made him a candidate member of
the Politburo in October 1977.

Not quite a super secretary as yet, although a serious contender
for the position since Brezhnev missed no opportunity to push him
into the limelight, he sent Chernenko abroad as the head of Party
delegations and arranged public appearances for him. One such ceremony was a "conference of Party leaders for Siberia and the Far East,"
which was held in 1978 at Krasnoyarsk, Chernenko's birthplace. On
July 11, appearing before thousands of *apparatchiki*, the heir apparent delivered an endless speech, a surprising feat for a leader not quite
at the top. He appeared masterful, expressing his emphatic opinion
on all subjects, scolding his audience, and praising Leonid Brezhnev
to the heavens, while conveying his "regards." Observers pointed out
that he devoted much of his speech to agriculture, which was his main
thrust.

What was Kulakov's reaction to this, since he was in theory
Chernenko's superior. Did he hear the bad news at the time? His
reaction remained unclear for many years. It was only at the news of
his death that rumors began to circulate in Moscow that Kulakov had
committed suicide. It was said that he had cut his veins. His death
was convenient for Chernenko in any event as it cleared the path for
him.

One further obstacle had to be overcome, however. Vigilant as
ever, Suslov tried to balance Brezhnev's overwhelming influence by
looking for someone better than Chernenko. Kulakov's death meant
he had to start his search again. Moreover the time factor became
important since an heir apparent cannot be groomed overnight. Did
Yuri Andropov perceive his ambition to the highest office in those
days? He had been head of the KGB for ten years and was universally known in the apparatus, having served as Central Committee
secretary for several years. This was very likely, but there was no
way of knowing how Suslov felt about Andropov's candidacy since
the latter really started his ascent to power in 1982 after Suslov's
death. Even so, the need remained to choose a younger pretender for
the next succession since Andropov was sixty-four years old in 1978.

It seemed obvious to Suslov that his colleague from Stavropol,

Mikhail Gorbachev, was the man for the job. His training and political ability as well as his background were well known to Suslov and Andropov. It seems that Suslov was reluctant, perhaps for reasons of ideological and social orthodoxy, to back sons of the intelligentsia or Stalin's *nomenklatura* as candidates to the highest offices. There were many such candidates in the middle ranks of the Party in the 1960s. In order to conform to traditions a leader had to be from a family unblemished by any suspicion of *kulak* or *gulag*, untouched by Stalin's repression, and also be of "proletarian" or of peasant origin. On all these counts Gorbachev was on top and his age was in his favor. In his advanced years, Brezhnev insisted on appointing as his successor another elderly man barely five years younger than himself. Suslov, along with the other non–Brezhnev leaders, proved more far sighted and chose a man of another generation.

Herein lies the key to Mikhail Gorbachev's future career: he stepped into Kulakov's shoes, not only as Secretary for Agriculture, but also as aspiring heir apparent, at least in the minds of those who were secretly preparing the way for him.

The "Summit" of Mineralnye Vody

How was it decided that Gorbachev should be given the supreme job? With hindsight it seems probable that the leaders made up their minds on September 19, 1978 at Mineralnye Vody, a spa at Stravopol. Brezhnev, accompanied by Chernenko, was on his way back from a visit to Azerbaidjan where he had met with Gaidar Aliev, the local leader and tool of the Secretary General, but who was subsequently Andropov's ally. The extraordinary convoy stopped at Krasnodar where they were greeted by First Secretary Medunev and Razumovsky, chairman of the regional executive council (*krayspolkom*). The group then headed for Mineralnye Vody where they were greeted by another Politburo member vactioning in the area, Yuri Andropov, who was accompanied by local leaders, including Mikhail Gorbachev. The meeting resulted in a "summit meeting" of the four General Secretaries: Brezhnev, Andropov, Chernenko, and Gorbachev. Although it was not made known to the people concerned, it can be assumed that Gorbachev's candidacy as Secretary of Agriculture was being considered. Medvedev accurately observed that the Brezhnev group had put forward another candidate, Ivan Bodiul, an agriculture expert who had worked alongside Brezhnev in Moldavia and served as a Party leader in the republic since 1961. Bodiul had been moved to

Moscow to be placed in charge of agriculture in the government as deputy chairman of the Council of Ministers. It appears that Suslov and Andropov put their case in rather emphatic terms or Mikhail Gorbachev must have sailed through his test with flying colors. In any case, he was elected Party Secretary at the following plenum two months later.

The compromise to appoint Gorbachev had not been reached, however, without Brezhnev receiving something in return. At the same plenum, Konstantine Chernenko, who had been candidate member for a year, became a full member. Another loyal follower of Brezhnev, Nikolai Tikhonov, was elected as candidate member, a first step toward taking over from Kosygin as Premier. Here is another example of Brezhnev's predilection for older men: Tikhonov, the future Soviet Premier, was seventy-four, a year younger than Kosygin.

Henceforth, Gorbachev was in charge of agriculture at the national level. It would be a mistake to assume that his activities ended there, for unlike Kulakov in the 1960s, who supervised the agriculture department of the Central Committee, he assumed firm control. The head of the department who had taken over from Kulakov in 1976, Vladimir Karlov, became his intermediary and retained the position until March 1987. Also, in 1979 Mikhail Gorbachev was appointed chairman of the commission for legislative proposals of the Chamber of Unions, one of the two chambers of the Supreme Soviet. This position usually goes to generalists among political leaders. (The next incumbents were Ligachev, later number two in the Party, then Nikolai Ryzkov, another Party secretary at the time, and Razumovsky, secretary in charge of cadres, followed.)

The Agriculture "Expert"

Finally, it became apparent that Mikhail Gorbachev's future was not linked to agriculture. The years from 1979 to 1983 when he was in charge were among the worst in regard to grain production in the USSR. In 1978 it had reached record levels with 230 million tons of cereals, to plunge to 179 milllion the following year, so that 31 million tons had to be imported, an amount greater than at any other time, before production went up slightly in 1980 to 189.1 million. Imports increased to 35 million despite President Carter's embargo on wheat exports to the USSR. The following year figures were so appalling that they were not disclosed. According to the State department's estimates, 150 million tons were harvested; imports were more easily assessed and broke all records: 46 million tons for the year 1981 alone. 1982 saw a slight improvement with production reaching 175 million tons, and no more than 32 million had to be imported.[2]

Honors had to rendered to the "expert" who announced, or rather "forecast" improvements each year. "Plans" as "scientific" as they were unrealistic were presented by the same expert: "between 238 and 243 million tons of yearly yield from 1982 to 1985, between 250 to 255 from 1986 to 1990" (Gorbachev's 1982 "food program"). He carefully relayed these predictions after 1981 to avoid blame for the failure, just as he distanced himself from the remedies advocated by Brezhnev and Chernenko since they both wanted to "throw money at the problem," in other words, invest massively in fertilizers, machinery, and irrigation without changing structures. After 1985, in his new role as General Secretary, Gorbachev tried to devise more flexible methods, but he is still to prove that he can extricate Soviet agriculture from its decline. At any rate, in the days of Brezhnev no one cast blame on him. Every harvest showed a worsening balance sheet for agriculture accompanied by fresh honors for the man in charge. One year to the day after his appointment as secretary Gorbachev ascended to the Politburo as candidate member on November 27, 1979. Just within three years he had climbed the three major rungs on his way to the top.

What was behind these favors? No doubt the protection of people who wished to redress the balance of power within the Politburo. Moreover, Gorbachev was seen as the only independent figure who managed not to antagonize the leaders on the opposite side. One should bear in mind that if Brezhnev had felt any aversion for Mikhail Gorbachev he would have stopped his progress, since he was well capable of doing so.

One observation can be made: it can be noted that Gorbachev's ascent coincided with that of Cernenko and some other Brezhnevites, obviously intended to counterbalance it. Already visible in 1978, this pattern recurred in 1979 since Gorbachev's appointment as candidate member of the Politburo was matched by Tikhonov's promotion to full member. In 1980, however, there was no corresponding measure since no Brezhnevite was promoted in that year either to the Politburo, except for the Byelorussian leader Kiselev who was made candidate member, nor to the secretariat. It appeared that Brezhnev's influence was on its way out.

From Stagnation to Fossilization

Moreover, since no one was able to alter the crumbling party and state structure it degenerated from stagnation to "fossilization." After Gorbachev's promotion in 1980 there was no other change in the leadership, not even at the Party Congress in the following year. It seemed as if the Politburo was frightened by having overreached itself after recruiting a younger man and had sealed its doors to all newcomers. It was agreed that it was a bold venture to appoint the new full member of the Politburo at the age of forty-nine, eight years younger than the youngest of his colleagues (Romanov) and twenty-one years younger than the others. The average age of the Politburo member was seventy in 1980. Even among the candidate members the youngest was Shervardnaze, who was four years older than Gorbachev. Among the secretaries the situation remained the same as it was after Gorbachev's accession—he was still eighteen years younger than most and eight years younger than Dolguikh, who was next in line, not to mention the super secretaries whose magic circle he had just joined along with Brezhnev, Suslov, Kirilenko, and Chernenko. Although the last was the youngest, still Gorbachev was twenty years younger than he!

Such was the absurdity of the situation, and nothing could be done but to wait. After 1982, the combined death of three full Politburo members within a little more than a year as well as three additional deaths before 1985—amounting to more than a third of the 1980 numbers—altered the balance considerably.

A Low Profile

What was to be done in the meantime? The best thing was to attract the least amount of notice, in other words, to keep away from the rivalries between the main contenders for power—those who, in spite of their years, thought they had a better chance than the next man because of the size of their clientele and the lobbies they could muster. On the one hand, there was Chernenko, a favorite with Brezhnev and his followers and, on the other, Kirilenko, one of the first empire builders of the Brezhnev era, with Suslov—with no ambition for himself—acting as umpire. Andropov stood on the sidelines and was preparing his attack from his KGB fortress.

The first to fall was Kirilenko. He was as old as Brezhnev and also a member of the Khrushchev Politburo of 1962. He had lost a lot of influence in the 1970s due to Kulakov's rise to power but more so to that of Chernenko who spared no effort in finishing him off. In 1979 several job changes made his major allies vulnerable, among whom could be called the "Sverdlovsk group." (In the 1950s Kirlenko was first secretary of this important industrial area of the Urals.) Yakov Ryabov, for example, Party secretary since 1976, had to give up this position in April 1979 to become first deputy chairman of Gosplan (State Planning Commission). Vitali Vorotnikov had been up to that time first deputy chairman of the Russian government and was sent into exile as ambassador to Cuba. Some of these men were later used by Andropov who selected many of Kirilenko's men for his first list of appointments.

After 1979, Chernenko lost his initiative. The Brezhnev group failed to promote any of its members into the top leadership, with the exception of Gorbachev. In the following year, Chernenko, chief organizer of the 26th Party Congress, did not miss the opportunity to square his accounts with his rival, Andropov. He was the only Politburo member not to chair a session, whereas Gorbachev enjoyed this privilege. However, those pinpricks made no difference to the congress being a "non–event" of no consequence and bringing no changes whatsoever in the leadership. Suslov's death in January 1982 tipped the scales in favor of Brezhnevites and opened the way for the succession, resulting in a downward turn for the prospects of Chernenko's group.

Brezhnev's Decline and Fall

Most of the events leading to the "end of reign" scandal, which burst upon Moscow at this time and was related at length to foreign correspondents by the KGB, are well known today. This was a juicy piece of news, implicating personalities ranging from Brezhnev's daughter Galina, Anatoli Kolevatev, manager of the Moscow Circus, Boris Burata, who was known as "Gypsy," an actor and big dealer, Anatoli Mikhov, a deputy minister of Culture and a first deputy-chairman of the KGB (related to Brezhnev), Semen Tsvigun, and to top it all off, the Kremlin kingmaker, Mikhail Suslov. In short, Brezhnev's daughter led a dissipated life which led her father to keep her away from Moscow. Her passion for a high life, for trips abroad and for diamonds gave her access to foreign countries. Under a false name she passed as a minor employee, such as make–up assistant, and went on several trips abroad and brought back foreign currency and precious stones. In January 1982 the KGB arrested several dealers who soon confessed to the circumstances leading to the "end of reign." The part played in the affair by Tsvigun, second in command of the KGB, who was put in charge of the investigation by Andropov, is still unclear. Did he try as a relative of Brezhnev to bury the affair? Or, under pressure from his superior Andropov, did he think that the scandal was too explosive and had to be dealt with openly? The second hypothesis seems more likely, just as it can be assumed that Suslov, who was concerned about Party unity and the leader's image, would have preferred to stop the proceedings. In any event, it arrived at a heated encounter between the two men by mid–January. Back home Tsvigun shot himself while Suslov suffered a massive heart attack. He died within a few days having nearly reached the age of eighty. The national funeral, which Brezhnev attended, was a welcome opportunity to arrest the main culprits of the "Circus gang," among whom were Boris the Gypsy. Since the move was given wide publicity by Brezhnev, it was a roundabout but nevertheless unmistakable way to show that the Brezhnev party was no longer immune and that its taste for high living had raised many eyebrows. After Brezhnev's death when an inventory was made of his estate, it was discovered that his collection of deluxe motorcars amounted to 44, mostly western, not to mention 120 decorations.

Andropov was not slow to take advantage of the situation. On May 21, 1982, with the title of party secretary, he stepped into Suslov's shoes as the man in charge of ideology. It gave him an unassailable position to block Chernenko's aspirations to power. The fascinating aspect of the few months immediately preceding Brezhnov's death and the unparalleled disarray striking the leader's group, with each of them a prey to disease and old age, they were reaping the fruits of their mistakes or corrupt practices now universally denounced. Thus, we see Brezhnev terminally ill in July, forced to witness the downfall of his lifelong protegé, the ever faithful Medunov, the first secretary at Krasnodar. When his end came on November 10, 1982, it only took two days for Andropov to become General Secretary, probably with the backing of Ustinov, the Defense Minister, Gromyko, Gorbachev, Kirilenko, Pelsho, and Romanov—in a word, all the Politburo "independents" against the members of the Brezhnev group (Tikhonov, Grishin, Kunaev, and possibly Shcherbitsky), who supported Chernenko. What was Gorbachev's attitude toward all this? As expected, he kept a low profile throughout the proceedings, although he was a super secretary and highly concerned with the struggle between his colleagues Andropov and Chernenko, it was quite out of the question that he should raise himself to their level. He pretended to be immersed in agriculture, but since the 1981 harvest proved even worse than the preceding ones he was careful not to attract too much attention in this field either. In May 1982, when the Party adopted one more program for increased production, the so-called "foodstuff program," he preferred to let Brezhnev himself wear the hat and introduce it to the plenum. Throughout 1982 he confined himself to commenting upon the documents in the provinces and to various conferences in the capital.

Andropov: The First Interregnum

The situation was different with Andropov in power. First of all, the new Secretary General had been his protector since the days of Stavropol, which happened to be his birthplace. Second, and perhaps more obvious, the number of super secretaries had decreased. Besides Andropov there were only Chernenko and Gorbachev, and it can be assumed which way the General Secretary's sympathies went. This became obvious in April 1983 when Gorbachev was chosen to present the customary report at the ceremony for Lenin's birthday.

Another unmistakable sign was the order of precedence during meetings of the Supreme Soviet. From time immemorial, Politburo members occupy three rows of benches—one behind the other—in the fashion of school benches, but perhaps slightly more comfortable. Each of the five seats of the three rows is significant, and the bench itself is of significance: a junior Politburo member would not dream of sitting in the front row, even though all the seats were not taken. In this respect a gap can be as important as a face on a photograph, and it becomes evident that a struggle for power is going on.

It was then on November 1982, just after Brezhnev's death, that Gorbachev was entitled only to a seat in the third row, far behind the five new incumbents on the first bench in the order of Andropov, Tikhenov, Chernenko, Ustinov, and Gromyko, and behind the middling personalities of the other bench were Shcherbitsky, Kunaev, Pelshe, and Grishin. (In this row there remained a gap which nobody dared fill as yet.) In June 1983, at the next meeting, Pelsho was dead and the two empty seats were taken by Romanov and Gorbachev. The latter had moved forward to the middle row for the first time, but remained in the last position. Six months later, in December 1983, there was another progression when Gorbachev occupied the first place in the row, just behind Andropov's seat, which was empty at the time.

This last progression did not mean that the way was wide open for the supreme leadership. In June, Romanov was still ahead of Gorbachev. Moreover the Leningrad Party leader was a Politburo member of longer standing than Gorbachev, and he had just been promoted to CC secretary on June 15. Therefore, he belonged to the group of super secretaries in the Secretariat, thereby limiting Gorbachev's influence. Did Andropov intend to isolate Romanov from his Leningrad base and neutralize him by appointing him to his new job? This was the KGB's version, which also circulated rumors on his wild living in Leningrad, especially on the occasion of his daughter's wedding when china made for Catherine the Great borrowed from the Hermitage was smashed by drunken guests. This might have been true, especially since the man selected to replace Romanov in Leningrad, Lev Zaykov, was not a close collaborator. As mayor of the city he was not the most likely candidate. Another significant detail must be pointed out: Gorbachev, not Romanov, presided over the inaugural ceremony of the new first secretary in Leningrad. This can only mean that henceforth the Stavropol official was not restricted to dealing with agriculture, and that he was involved in cadre promotions.

Even so, it was a curious way for Andropov to undermine Gorbachev's rival by making him a candidate for the supreme leadership. Romanov remained in the limelight for a while under Andropov. During a meeting with the old Bolshevik guard in August, one of Andropov's last appearances, he was accompanied by two men only, Romanov and Gorbachev. The former was given the seat to the right of Andropov. In November it was Romanov who read the official report on the occasion of the solemn Party meeting to mark the anniversary of the revolution. We should also bear in mind that in September there was a denouncement in *Izvestia* of the Ipatovo method—to the great embarrassment of Gorbachev and his Stavropol colleagues.

Starting in December the situation changed. Andropov had remained confined to his hospital bed and Gorbachev was supposed to have been chosen to convey his directives to the Politburo. It is also possible that the ex-KGB chief left both candidates to his succession active in the field to prevent Chernenko from succeeding him.

The Second Interregnum: Chernenko or the Farce

If that was Andropov's intention, it did not succeed, and in fact the rivalry between the two men paved the way for Chernenko. Andropov died too soon, before either Romanov or Gorbachev had been able to consolidate their positions. A split in the voting between the two candidates who were opposed to the Brezhnev group—or perhaps a compromise reached on the initiative of Ustinov and Gromyko, both of whom retained in their old age a measure of authority—ensured that Chernenko was declared secretary general. After an exceptionally lengthy debate after Andropov's death lasting four days, Chernenko's position was ratified by a plenum as Secretary General on February 9, 1981. There were obvious rifts in what was considered the "leadership." Dev Muraka, who lived in Moscow at the time, came up with a theory which makes sense in the light of subsequent developments. In order to placate both the Brezhnev faction, unwilling to eclipse itself and the somewhat senile vanity of Chernenko, who had insisted on getting the job Brezhnev had chosen him for, that wish was granted, but only on three conditions: (1) Andropov's policies should be continued, (2) the men he appointed should remain in power, and (3) Mikhail Gorbachev would be Chernenko's second-in-command and heir apparent, at least implicitly.[3] The new interregnum was too short and colorless to speculate whether the first condition was fulfilled, but the other two were honored. There were no changes in the leadership throughout 1984, that is apart from the death of Dimitri Ustinov in December.

Without any doubt Mikhail Gorbachev became second-in-command. At the March plenum when Chernenko's appointment as General Secretary was ratified, he spoke in support of collective decisions in the name of the "younger" leaders, thereby giving the indication that he was from that point on their representative. The intervention became known only later when a pamphlet on sale several days after the event had been reported in the daily newspapers. In addition, a Soviet television news reporter made sure it was seen on the screen with the name of the speaker clearly visible. During the following month, Gorbachev was made chairman of the foreign affairs commission in the Chamber of Union of the Supreme Soviet, a seat to which secretaries for ideology are entitled, previously occupied by Suslov, Andropov, and Chernenko. Agriculture was now definitely a thing of the past. In any event, the Chernenko interregnum was of a shorter duration than the one with Andropov so that it will be remembered as a caricature of fossilized gerontocracy. From the very first week the political Moscow chronicle was reduced to the usual speculations of the leader's health, but in a more extreme form. Everything appeared to be at a standstill. The rare speeches that Chernenko did manage to deliver—with great difficulty—were of no interest to anyone. It is now clear that this new installment of a sham succession was a mistake.

Despite the facts, Mikhail Gorbachev was aware of public expectancy or felt more self-confident, he came to occupy a central position nevertheless. In domestic policy he moved away from agriculture to subjects of more general interest and even made some daring speeches. For example, at an address to Party ideologists in December 1984, which was not published in full, he spoke of "*glasnost*" (transparency) and attacked "conservatism, indifference and stagnation." This last word (*zastoy*) is the one he used later to describe the Brezhnev era. Several years later in his book on *perestroika*, Gorbachev insisted—perhaps because he had been blamed for keeping quiet under Brezhnev—that he had fought hard and long before his assumption to power:

> We adopted the notion of *perestroika* not only for pragmatic interests and considerations, but in answer to pangs of conscience . . . after a search of theoretical nature to improve our knowledge of society had spurred us into action.

Some factors contributing to those "theoretical researches" must have been analyses of the "overall situation of the economy" which had been carried out, added Gorbachev, by "Party and State officials" before the April 1985 plenum when Gorbachev's doctrines first came to light. However, the process of maturation had started earlier. In the words of the writer:

> In my report of April 22, 1983 at the Lenin anniversary meeting, I quoted Leninist principles on the need to take account of objective economic laws, on planning and independent accounting, on making intelligent use of marketing surveys, of material and moral incentives. The audience gave an enthusiastic reception to these evocations of Lenin's doctrine. I knew then that my thoughts were on the same lines as the preoccupations of Party comrades and many people in the country. . . . . Yes, many comrades felt an acute need

for social renewal. Though I must confess that I also experienced other reactions to my speech—not everyone was in agreement—I had been less optimistic than I should have been (*Perestroika*, pp. 20–21 of the Russian edition).

This is a significant revelation on two counts. First, because no one had noticed those "daring words" at the time, and the account of the meeting given on the pages of *Pravda* on April 23, 1983 made no mention of any quotations from Lenin being rapturously received. Second, because Brezhnev had already died, and in spite of Andropov's being in power any idea of renewal seemed unpopular. This may explain why—neither in this book nor in his report on the occasion of the 70th anniversary of the revolution in November 1987—Gorbachev failed to name his predecessor and protector.

Gorbachev soon had opportunities to influence foreign policy since Brezhnev's stagnation had produced disastrous results. In October 1983, the deployment of NATO's "Euromissiles" in several Western European countries was a serious blow to Soviet prestige. Andropov answered it by futile and feeble verbal protests. All disarmament negotiations were suspended. In addition, the destruction by a Soviet military aircraft of a South Korean 747 Boeing high above Sakhalin Island in the Pacific, caused international consternation when 269 passengers and crew aboard the plane flying from Anchorage to Seoul, South Korea, died meaninglessly on August 31–September 1, 1983. The tragedy put the USSR in the dock and raised many eyebrows, even in Moscow, not so much for humanitarian reasons as for security. Anti–aircraft defense took hours to spot the airplane above the forbidden zone of Kamchatka and Sakhalin and the Soviet pilot fired at it without really identifying his target.

In spite, or perhaps because of, the increasingly overpowering presence of Andrei Gromyko as head of Soviet diplomacy, the need for a new approach was felt. Mikhail Gorbachev tried his hand cautiously at foreign affairs, and with some success. In June 1984 in a speech in Smolensk, he vehemently attacked American policy. But he managed to include a sentence to the effect that "detente could not be taken as a thing of the past." In view of subsequent events, it is likely that he favored a resumption of dialogue and pressed for it in debates between Politburo members. A wish was given some substance when Gromyko visited Washington in September and later, in January 1955, when he met with the Secretary of State in Geneva. In an address to his electors in Feburary 1985, Gorbachev also advocated a less exclusive preoccupation with the United States and more attention paid to Europe and Japan. All the same, he was careful not to attack current policies openly. For example, while staying in Sofia in September—at a time when Moscow was attempting to dissuade its satellites from initiating detente, and when Honecker, the East German leader, had just been forbidden to pay a visit to West Germany—he pressed President Zhivkov of Bulgaria to give up his planned visit to Bonn.

This being the case, Gorbachev was ready to take advantage of the fact that he was one of the few Soviet leaders able to travel and project a different image abroad. He had already been to Canada in 1983 as head of a parliamentary delegation and made a favorable impression on his hosts. In June 1984 he went to Italy for the funeral of the communist leader Berlinguer, and in December 1984 he and Raisa undertook a tremendously successful journey to Great Britain. The emergence of the Gorbachev couple among Soviet leaders was by then commented upon in foreign countries. Politicians were eager to meet them, and Margaret Thatcher's words made headlines when she commented: "This is someone I could do business with." After each trip Gorbachev was widely considered as a future Kremlin leader. Although he could be as evasive as any Soviet politician in reply to British MP's denunciations of violations of human rights in the USSR, he could also answer honestly while applying the policy of *glasnost* long before it was in general use. Thus, he announced to journalists the death of Defense Minister Marshal Ustinov before the official communiqué was issued. This event caused him to return from London sooner than expected in order to prepare for the final stage of the succession struggle.

The Last Card of the Brezhnev Faction: Grishin

At home the situation was fluid. In October 1981, Chernenko had convened the last plenum of the Central Committee to launch another huge investment program in agriculture. This was not in keeping with Gorbachev's ideas, since he had long been convinced that a solution would not be found without a reform in management. As in the program on foodstuffs in 1982, the heir apparent chose to keep out of the proceedings. The report was presented by Tikhanov, and Gorbachev remained silent. This goes to show that he was not on safe ground, and there were indications that some people were maneuvering to take over from Chernenko who was moribund by then. On October

18, 1984 the fact did not go unnoticed that Romanov achieved prominence in an official photograph of the ceremony at which Gromyko was awarded a decoration. He was closer to the team of gerontocrats—Chernenko, Tikhanov, and Gromyko—than Gorbachev. Two months later, Romanov was chairing the commission to organize Ustinov's funeral. It must be added that the ex–boss of Leningrad was involved in armament industries which were of primary importance to the defense minister.

However, an outsider began to push his way to the front during the early months of 1985 while Chernenko was agonizing. If anyone was trying to delay the demise of the old guard and find an alternative to Gorbachev, there was no hope of finding a suitable super secretary, except for Romanov whose popularity had slumped after a brief revival in the autumn. Only Viktor Grishin, First City Secretary in Moscow, could be eligible. He was a colorless figure and a typical representative of the Stalin–Brezhnev *nomenklatura* executives. According to Medvedev, his son was married to Beria's illegitimate daughter. He had been on the Politburo since 1971, and although he was not in the Secretariat, as leader of the largest party organization in the country, his political weight was considerable. His age (seventy in 1984) made him more credible than Gorbachev with the old guard, who did not feel threatened by him. He also seemed to be in fairly good physical shape. In any event, Grishin was very visible during the elections of the Russian Supreme Soviet in February 1985. Taking advantage of the fact that the ailing Chernenko constituency was in his city, the Moscow Party chief campaigned hard on behalf of the Secretary General. He presided over the ceremony of "casting votes" in a specially appointed hospital room as well as at the reception of his mandate by the sick leader a few days later. This was the last time Chernenko was seen in public.

This maneuvering was, however, nothing more than a last ditch effort. Gorbachev had plenty of influential backers. Following information released by *Pravda*'s editor–in–chief Afanasiev, it was widely rumored in Moscow that Gorbachev was not only second–in–command but that he also exercized "supreme power." Some time later Gromyko revealed that Gorbachev now chaired Politburo meetings The make-up of the Politburo had also changed since Brezhnev's days since Andropov had introduced three new members in 1982 and 1983, two of whom did not belong to the faction of the deceased leader—Mikhail Solomentsev and Vitali Vorotnikov. (In the case of Gaidor Aliev, who was elected immediately after Brezhnev's death, doubts remain whether he was Andropov's client.) Generally speaking, Grishin could count on his own vote, that of the old Premier Tikhonov, on Kunaev, and probably Romanov, who also preferred the temporary rule of Brezhnev's sort rather than the long–term leadership of Gorbachev.

In the "sparsely populated" Politburo of March 1985—only ten full members after Chernenko's death—Grishin commanded a large minority, especially since Shcherbitsky was away in California at the time and was unable to take part in the debates. Naturally some leaders were more influential than others, including some who officially did not belong to the Grishin group. For example, Chebrikov, chairman of the KGB, who was only a candidate member at the time, became a full member a few weeks later, probably for services rendered. He is supposed to have been responsible for blocking Romanov's way and then made Grishin's candidacy hopeless by threatening to make disclosures about past malversations by Moscow city managers.

Gromyko's Role

Gromyko was another key figure in the election of the supreme leader, the only member of the old team left after Ustinov's and Chernenko's deaths. A rumor circulated that he supported Gorbachev. A first indication of this was the publicity given to Gorbachev by the Foreign Ministry in the February elections when its press bureau invited foreign correspondents to the polling station where the future Party chief was voting. Another sign was the curious story supposedly disclosed by an official of the Central Committee, Leonid Dobrokhotov, to an American during an American–Soviet meeting in August 1987, later published it in the *Spectator* magazine on September 19, 1987. Dobrokhotov did not describe Gorbachev's election by the Central Committee but only the first stage of the process that takes place in the Politburo. The way the decision of the supreme body was greeted by the Central Committee's officials—in other words by the *apparatchiki*—and was allegedly as follows:

> The officials of the Central Committee were gathering in the waiting rooms, grouped according to their preferences. Half of them were in favor of Grishin while the other half were for Gorbachev. There was a great deal of tension in the group. Many walked frantically about smoking one cigarette after another. The voting was close, and finally Gorbachev won, thanks to a vote by Gromyko who was chairing the meet-

ing. Five minutes later another Central Committee member arrived and announced abruptly: "Comrades, the new General Secretary is Comrade Gorbachev." Dobrokhotov remembered that half the Central Committee's officials nearly jumped for joy and the other half could hardly contain their disappointment.

Thus, Gromyko played a major role in Gorbachev's election, although it did not turn out to his advantage. The old man of diplomacy was at the height of his power throughout the years of Brezhnev's decline and galloping gerontocracy. He had demonstrated it on several occasions in 1983 when he obstructed several of Andropov's initiatives on the Euromissiles, and again in 1984 when he openly scolded Chernenko in the presence of foreign representatives. His obvious ambition was to break all historical records as diplomatic head of a great power, in the manner of Metternich or Nesselrode in the last century.

He probably thought that a leader of the younger generation would need his experience. Instead, in the following few months he lost his job in exchange for a purely honorific title as President. This disappointment led him to look more kindly on the candidate that he had helped to defeat in March of 1985. When Grishin found himself dismissed from his Moscow Party job and looking for something to do, Head of State Andrei Gromyko appointed him "State Counselor with the Presidium of the Supreme Soviet." In this capacity Grishin was entitled to attend the 27th Congress the following spring, although simply as a delegate.[4] He was a counselor in 1987,[5] when the corruption of the Moscow leaders was exposed by Yeltsin, Grishin's successor and a radical leader of the Gorbachev reform movement. The Soviet press repeatedly linked the corrupt dealings of the City Soviet with those of the diplomatic institutes under the authority of the Foreign Ministry. Similarly, Anatoli Grishchenko, head man of the "Gromyko faction" in charge of the Party Committee at the ministry, was reprimanded by the new Moscow leaders late in 1986.

Another indication of the Gromyko–Grishin connection was Murarka's report that Grishin, when he saw that his candidacy was opposed in the Politburo debates by Chebrikov and some others, put forward Andrei Gromyko's candidacy as Secretary General. The fact that on March 12, 1985 the Foreign Minister presented Gorbachev as elected leader to the plenum of the Central Committee, which had to ratify the Politburo decision, is not really meaningful. After all, Andropov's appointment had been "hailed" in November 1982 by his rival Chernenko whose own appointment was greeted in similar fashion fifteen months later by Gorbachev in person. Persistent rumors have it that another Politburo speaker, Kunaev—a full blooded Brezhnevite—heaped the most lavish praises on the new master. He also lived to regret the day.

Of greater interest are the contents of Gromyko's speech published as a pamphlet a few days later. Only a few copies were printed. Before quoting large excerpts of the only example of the personality cult applied to the new Soviet leader, it should be pointed out that Gromyko refers to the Politburo and its collective wisdom several times. The paragraphs in which he "speaks for himself" are clearly indicated. On the other hand, there is no trace of the sentence which became famous: "The man smiles pleasantly but his teeth are made of steel." However, the text speaks for itself:

Mikhail Gorbachev is fully versed in Party affairs. . . . It is no exaggeration to say that his qualifications are outstanding. The Politburo has pointed out that he is a man of principle, with strong convictions. I can testify to this in person. He expresses his position directly, whether it be agreeable to the other person or not.

It was remarked at the Politburo meeting that Mikhail Gorbachev is far sighted and sharp minded. . . . There are many questions which are difficult to examine in black and white terms; there may be other colors, decisions in between. Mikhail Gorbachev can always find such solutions, in keeping with the Party line.

One also has to add this, which is more evident to me because of my office than to other comrades. He can grasp entirely and immediately the essence of the changes that occur outside our country on the international stage. I have often been struck by his capacity to immediately and fully understand all the implications of a subject. . . . Mikhail Gorbachev is an eminently erudite person through his training and his work experience. . . . This man can approach problems analytically; he is brilliant in this respect.

The conclusion reached by the Politburo is the right one. We have found in Mikhail Gorbachev an exceptional and outstanding personality who will admirably fit the position of Secretary General of the Central Committee of the CPSU.[6]

Was the Vote Unanimous?

Several observers rightly commented on the somewhat unusual formula employed in the Central Committee's communiqué announcing Mikhail Gorbachev's "unanimous" election. The Russian language has two words to express the idea: the first is *edinoglasno*, meaning "in one voice" (from the stem *glas* or *golas*, voice, which appears in *glasnost*), corresponding closely to what happens in voting when "not one vote" is cast against the candidate. This is the way the results of voting legislative measures by the Supreme Soviet are announced, after the chairman of the meeting has made sure no one voted against him. The second word, *edinodushno* literally means "with one soul" (*dusha*). It is less precise than the former, describing more a consensus situation where a large majority is obtained, allowing for minority dissenting votes. Thus, when the Soviet press reports election results to the Supreme Soviet, it states that deputies were elected *edinodushno* and (not *edinoglasno*), meaning by a large majority (98 or 99 percent). They allow a few fractions of a point to be left to last minute ditchers.

Andropov's election in 1982 and that of Chernenko in 1984 were announced as *edinoglasno*. However, Gorbachev was elected *edinodushne*, the very word used by Gromyko to describe the situation in the Politburo. Someone must have voted against him.

Even so, if such opposition really existed, it was defeated handsomely. The hasty way the succession was dealt with indicates that the most important decisions had been made previously, while Chernenko was still agonizing. He died on March 9 after 7:00 in the evening. The very next day—prior to the official anouncement and after Gromyko had carried out his engagements in the usual fashion and held talks with his French colleague, Roland Dumas—the Central Committee's plenum elected Gorbachev in his place. Allowing for delays in sending out invitations and difficulties in travelling to Moscow, it is probable that some members failed to attend. The proceedings were made public the same evening, so that on the following day *Pravda* presented a portrait of Mikhail Gorbachev on the front page, with the news of Chernenko's demise in the middle pages. Since Khrushchev's fall in 1964 the succession had never been so swift. The old adage, "The king is dead, long live the king" had never been so apt as it was then.

Chapter V

THE GENERAL SECRETARY

Even a leader belonging to the highest circles of power sees enormous changes in his status on the day when he becomes General Secretary of the Soviet Communist Party, more changes than upon entering the Holy of Holies of the Politburo, an aim of every leader.

The reason is that the head of the Communist party, although he is only expressing the views of the collegiate leadership, is the official spokesman of the ruling group. He is the only one given prominence by the communications media since all important or less important decisions are announced in his name. Every speech, message, or telegram of his is given wide publicity. For example, everything that Mikhail Gorbachev said or did since March 11, 1985 has been reported on the front page of *Pravda* in full and in his name. Until then he could only expect a shortened version containing no visible headlines on the inside pages of the Party daily. Similarly his speeches are produced live on television, and are on the front pages of *The Party Life*, the official weekly. The media ignore other top leaders or pay much less attention to them. Despite other reforms all of these practices have been maintained under the new regime.

Another expression of the predominant role of the Secretary General can be seen in his announcements of major initiatives taken in foreign policy by attending in person summit meetings and granting audiences to foreign visitors. Past Soviet history proves that the leading role in diplomacy cannot be taken for granted: Khrushchev had to share it with his Prime Minister Bulganin for several years; Brezhnev did the same for almost seven years with Kosygin until 1971 when he took over directly. Hence controlling foreign policy is a means for the leader to consolidate his authority. It is the best way to gain publicity either abroad or in the USSR. Gorbachev was well aware of this when he immediately replaced Gromyko with one of his trusted friends and took over the most visible part of his duties.

The position of Secretary General gives him the right to initiate and stimulate action. In theory this function is limited since the Secretary General—contrary to popular belief—has no special prerogatives in the Politburo; he is only *primus inter pares* within the team. (For this reason the formula used in the days of the personality cult was "Politburo headed by Comrade X," is contrary to the statutes.) He may also find himself in the minority. Even so, he chairs the weekly meetings, traditionally figures in newspaper reports at the top of the list of members, and last but not least, coordinates and organizes the daily work of the Party secretariat. This is an executive organ which prepares Politburo decisions and implements their application. In more general terms, insofar as he is spokesman for the leadership, the Secretary General is the only leader who can take bold initiatives, alter old patterns, and affect changes. The others are only entitled to interpret—sometimes in their own way—the leader's directives and clarify their method of application in specific sectors. Above all, since nobody is above him, by definition the Party leader is "on the last lap of his career," less self–interested than others. He can, like Brezhnev, watch over his assets, increase his own prosperity and that of fellow leaders. On the other hand, he may cherish the ambition of making his mark on history and lead the country to fuller accomplishments. This is the direction that Mikhail Gorbachev intended to take, and it becomes clearer with each passing year in power.

At first Gorbachev had to watch his step. As in Washington, Paris, and in many other Western capitals, similar to any other president, he announced loudly that he was going "to change things," follow a more judicious policy than his predecessor, and in short, apply the "program" or the "platform" on which he was elected. Nothing of the sort is applicable in Moscow where the new Secretary General represents the old collegiate leadership and is kept under close watch. Stepping out of line can still be fatal to the leader. Besides, since the Party is supposed never to err, it is imperative to proclaim that everything will continue as usual. Sure enough, in his inaugural speech at the April 1985 plenum, Mikhail Gorbachev declared "the strategy established by the 26th Party Congress and by the CC plenums that followed will be pursued." In view of the fact that in 1984 the 26th Congress is the archetype of Brezhnevian "non–events," the program is far from exciting. Of course, the new leader added that the "Leninist interpretation" of continuity signifies an "irrepressible march forward" and "overcoming any obstacle to development." All the same, the speeches during his first year—1985—do not bear the stamp of originality.

Not until the 27th Congress in February 1986 did the Secretary General begin to advocate his own ideas. They went in several directions: he criticized his predecessors, and especially Brezhnev. This gave him an opportunity to outline his own plan of "restructuring," soon to be called *perestroika*; then came "transparency" (*glasnost*). As supreme leaders in the USSR mostly make use of the spoken word as an instrument of power, the best way to study his intentions is to analyze the numerous speeches (a thick volume) delivered in his first two years of power.

Brezhnev Under Accusation

It was easy to predict that Brezhnev would soon come in for criticism, as did every Soviet Party leader before him, despite declarations of continuity. Leaders have always been eager to revise their predecessors' policies—or at least their "excesses." Thus, "destalinization" was followed by "dekhrushchevization"; that "debrezhnevization" was to follow was obvious since the shortcomings of the previous period, encompassing consvervatism, stagnation and dogmatism, were there for all to see. However, in Moscow it takes a bold man to open doors that are already wide open. After all, was not Gorbachev a full member of the past leadership? All the same, the abcess had to be lanced and the ground on which the Brezhnev faction was discredited had to be prepared. Still it was not until the 27th Congress that the Secretary General started to lift the veil from stagnation, although still in general terms, when he stated:

> For some years now, the effect of Party and State organizations has been to slow down necessary developments. . .
> . The problems caused by the country's advance multiplied faster than the solutions proposed. Inertia, immobilism in the structures, and outdated methods of management, loss of dynamism of the work force, and an ever present bureaucracy, all contributed to the worsening of the situation. Society has been overcome by stagnation. Changes were absolutely necessary, but a curious attitude prevailed throughout the central organizations and at the grass root level.

The aim was to improve matters without changing anything. This cannot be done, comrades![1]

The word "stagnation" (*zastoi*) came out, and was to remain in the forefront for a long time. Soon afater the plenum of January 1987, *Pravda* paved the way by publishing an article on Brezhnev's anniversary criticizing him severely. Gorbachev felt confident enough to do the same, but more thoroughly:

> In the course of the last five year plan, social problems have been increasingly ignored in economic life, a kind of blindness has struck them. . . . Parasitism has developed and a wave of consumerism has arisen. An indication of a decline in moral values is an increase in drunkenness, drug addiction, and a rise in the crime rate.[2]

All this has taken its toll in the ranks of the Party.

> The principle of equality between communists was often violated. Many Party members who exercized important functions found themselves outside any control and immune to criticism. . . . Some of them became accomplices or even instigators of criminal actions. The process manifested itself in rather monstrous shapes due to moral decay of cadres and infringement of socialist legality, especially in Uzbekistan, Moldavia, Turkmenistan, in several areas of Kazakhstan, in Krasnodar territory, the region of Rostov, in Moscow, etc. Our primary task is to restore the image of clean living and honest leadership, an image which has been tainted by the crimes of a group of degenerates.[3]

The terms "degenerates" and "monstrous violations" are indeed strong. After all, corruption had been denounced before Gorbachev when Andropov had taken the first steps in this direction. A more novel approach was criticizing moral standards among the top leaders, especially in the Central Committee:

> Let us be candid. For years now a whole range of burning problems have been left out of the agenda of the plenum. Our comrades remember that the CC plenums used to be held after hurried preparation as a mere formality. Many members of the CC were incapable throughout the terms of their office in participating in the debates let alone submitting proposals.[4]

In this context Gorbachev quoted a plenum which was held in 1970 or 1971 on the very question which he put forward after 1985—technological advance in industry. But the debate never took place because the leadership blanched at the enormity of the task. The most vivid description of this chaos is shown in Gorbachev's address to a group of writers on June 19, 1986:

> One day Brezhnev said it was necessary to organize a plenum on scientific and technical matters. I was shown files of documents that had been prepared for that purpose. When they started to look at them they suddenly realized that they did not know what to do with them, nor where to put them. So the papers were set aside.[5]

Let us now come back to the January plenum showing the Politburo and the top leadership just as helpless as the Central Committee, with economic reforms the least of their concerns:

> There were huge numbers of decorations, awards, titles, and bonuses distributed, and numerous birthdays were celebrated in the outlying regions as well as in the center. The gap between the daily realities and the euphoric make believe would become wider than ever . . .[6]

Naturally each leader was reluctant to give up his cozy job. Evoking the need to "deal in due course with the problem of mature cadres," in other words, to cut out the dead wood, Gorbachev added:

> Violation of this natural principle led, at one stage, to a lowering in the working capacity of the Politburo, the Secretariat and the Central Committee as a whole as well as its apparatus, along with that of the government. As a matter of fact, comrades, a large part of the Secretariat was renewed shortly after the April [1985] plenum, in the same way as the heads of departments of the CC. Practically the entire presidium of the Council of Ministers was replaced. This was necessary since for a long time the Central Committee and the government had been virtually at a standstill. . . . This cannot and must not happen again.[7]

Perestroika

The extent of changes of cadres initiated by Gorbachev will be shown later. From the start he made use of his criticism of general policies to introduce what was to be called, in the USSR and abroad, *perestroika* (restructuring).

When did the word first appear? Almost at once, but in the early stages it applied to a few changes in the economy. At the April 1985 plenum, just a month after his assumption of power, the Secretary General announced that he intended to "fully restructure the work of the top echelons of economic management."[8] In June of the same year, the word made its appearance in his plea for "a thorough restructuring of planning and management of the whole economic machine."[9] Until then it had been used only as an adjunct to the slogan of the day as the theme of a conference of managers held in the Kremlin: "Stepping up scientific and technical progress." The scope became wider in the summer of 1985 when the new leader said in an interview with *Time* magazine that "it is essential for all of us, in all areas, to restructure."[10]

In fact it was not until the Party Congress and after the summer of 1986 that the call for *perestroika* became nationwide. The first full definition was given in July of that year in a speech delivered at Khaborovsk, in the Soviet Far East:

> *Perestroika* as it stands now does not merely apply to economics but to all the other aspects of social life: social relations, political systems, ideology and moral attitudes, to the profile of the Party and all our cadres and their approach to work. . . . I would like to equate the words restructuring and revolution. Our changes, our reforms, are a real revolution in the whole system of social relations, in the minds and hearts of people.[11]

Again, in January 1987, *perestroika* was defined:

> Restructuring rests on the living creativity of the masses, it seeks the manifold development of democracy and socialist self–management, it encourages private initiative, independent action, a strengthening of discipline and order, more widespread transparency (*glasnost*), criticism and self–criticism in every area, it means a deeper respect for the value and dignity of human beings.[12]

In other words, *perestroika* is all things to all men. From this time on Gorbachev took a "leap forward" in his concepts, and *perestroika* acquired three distinct meanings: it concerned everyone, not only the Party summit; it did not undermine the value of "socialism," but sought to exploit it to better advantage; and finally, it required a sustained effort over a long period.

On the first point, Gorbachev explained what he had in mind at a speech in Krasnadar in September 1986:

> My firm belief is that people are aware today that restructuring is a serious business. Not long ago it was thought that only the upper reaches of society were involved—it was up there that a change in the leaders' behavior had to take place. Now people know that all of society, each individual citizen, has to be restructured.[13]

Naturally, it is an urgent necessity and not a mere wish. This became the rallying cry from January 1987 on:

> We envisage really revolutionary changes in society in all sectors. Such a radical step is inevitable, simply because there is no other way. We have no right to retreat, and there is nowhere to retreat.[14]

Perestroika was based on socialist principles, and Gorbachev insisted too often on this assertion, which in time appeared as a sign of weakness, since no Secretary General should be forced to give communist guarantees to opponents of his policies. From the very beginning he made his position clear. In July 1986 at Khabarovsk he said:

> We must not search for answers to our problems outside the confines of socialism but within our system. . . . This is not to everyone's liking in the West. They always hope over there for a sign that socialism will be relinquished, that we will bow down to capitalism and adopt its ways.[15]

The tone was even firmer when he touched on transparency:

> *Glasnost* and democracy, . . . no permissiveness is meant here. Transparency is intended to strengthen socialism . . . [and] there is no question of undermining socialism or its values. . . . There is one criterion, comrades: more socialism, more democracy. All solutions of the new problems have to be found within socialism, not outside.[16]

Whether or not it remained under the ideological umbrella, *perestroika* was an open—ended process of long duration, and it met with greater obstacles:

> We have to realize that we have only reached the preliminary stage of restructuring. The main effort, which is one of a

highly complex nature, lies ahead of us.[17]

Again, three months later, Gorbachev claimed:

We must hold out together another two or three tough years
in which we shall have to solve simultaneously, as we go
along, enormous problems, create the necessary conditions,
in politics and economics, in the administration, in judiciary,
moral and psychological attitudes, for restructuring. . . .
This may prove to be a most stressful period, but also the
most interesting.[18]

However, a few months later the duration of hardship had length-
ened, when he explained:

How long will *perestroika* take? This is difficult to answer.
Not two or three years for sure, but much longer. We shall
direct all our efforts toward a painstaking enterprise which
will lead our motherland across new frontiers by the end of
the twentieth century.[19]

Radical Reform in the Economy

The first field of application in which *perestroika* was applied was
the economy. This is where anomalies were most visible, and where
the Party saw its greatest opportunity. Before launching a campaign
for *glasnost*, it was imperative to boost up industry and agriculture
and to make the system more efficient in order to sustain production
and make the country stronger. In a way, democratization, soon
called for by the Secretary General, was dependent on this basic task
of restructuring.

The concrete proposals for wide reforms were revealed at the
June 1987 plenum. However, the Secretary General had made his
views known even earlier. It should be remembered that the word
perestroika was used in April 1985 in the context of economic reforms.
From the very beginning, Mikhail Gorbachev was careful not to be
bogged down by a few "experiments," in selected industrial firms and
sectors which aimed at greater autonomy, improved planning, and es-
tablishing "direct links" between producers and consumers. Whether
they were successful did not matter since they were no more than
experiments. In general, managers and workers disliked them and attempted to drag their feet, or do nothing about them. Such was the
situation in the early 1980s, and it could have remained the same for

the next twenty years. However, the new Party chief had something quite different in mind, as he made it clear at his first plenum: "The time has come to stop experimenting and create a coherent system of management."[20] He used the same blunt approach in another speech in June of the same year, this time crossing his t's and dotting his i's:

> If we carry on repeating, for one, two or three years, that we are conducting an experiment, that we have extended it to two or three new sectors of industry, and if we fail to devise at the same time a comprehensive system of economic management, the situation will not improve. . . . Obviously the obstacle lies in being afraid of making a mistake, being reluctant to make drastic changes, sometimes out of sheer conservatism. Today, because of this, we are faced with the same problems as several decades back, but in a more acute form.[21]

Gorbachev prepared the reforms that he was to announce in concrete terms two years later: a really new system of management, which should bear results "during the 12th five–year plan," that is before 1990. The task was enormous. There were hundreds of topics open to debate between conservatives and reformists, staunch ideologists and "modernists" who would have like to imitate the West, between intellectuals and passive bureaucrats, and the weight of habits was immense. A description of the major difficulties makes this confession clearer.

To begin with, the long–established characteristics of the Soviet economy stand in the way of reform. Bureaucracy, lack of enterprise, and difficulties in applying theoretical research, which is of the highest quality, to industrial purposes, all contribute to technological backwardness, poor quality of goods, and shoddy services. This applies to industry as well as agriculture. It is even more difficult to remedy the consequences of delays in agriculture. Crops, which are left in the fields since there are no lorries to collect them for over a week, are ruined, while in factories it is not possible to make up for lost time at the end of the month or year. However, in both cases results are disastrous. Nonetheless, workable remedies are well known. Less stress must be placed on fulfilling the Plan so that firms acquire more autonomy; the concept of profitability, competition, and gain must be restored even if this seems to be flirting with a market economy.

Unfortunately all these ideas were discussed before and were even used in the past with no success. Thus the concept of "financial autonomy" for individual enterprises (the Russian word is *khozrashchet* meaning "economic accounting") is a key word in Gorbachev language. It was already discussed under Brezhnev, especially at the time of timid reforms attempted by Kosygin in 1965, under Khrushchev and even Stalin. It was seen as a useful means of accountability to measure success or failure of enterprises. Real financial independence was another matter. Even Gorbachev treads carefully in this area. But he did go as far as acknowledging that some firms might go bankrupt in exceptional circumstances.

No far–reaching innovations were proposed for reforming administrative services in the economic sector in 1985. Gorbachev eliminated a number of agricultureal ministries whose responsibilities were assumed by the Governmental Committee of Agro–industry. However, he does not dare to do the same to a dozen engineering ministries. They are only combined to form a "bureau" of the Council of Ministers. The Chernobyl disaster made him set up a new ministry in charge of nuclear energy, but all other relevant administrative bodies continue in conjuction with it. Overall the Soviet government consists of over ninety ministeries among which at least ten serve specific sectors of industry: civil engineering, metal works, agriculture, and transport. To this must be added dozens of corresponding ministries in the fifteen republics of the Federation whose cabinets are often as large as the whole of the French government put together, including over fifty ministries throughout the Ukraine, Kazakhstan, and in the Russian Republic.

More daring were changes affecting foreign trade. This ministry, since Lenin gave it a "monolopy on foreign trade," was not only savagely purged but it was also reduced in size. The old minister, Palelichev, was retired; one of his deputies was arrested and sentenced for corruption and many were dismissed. A "Commission for External Economic Relations," headed by a vice–premier, now coordinates the activities of all the bodies concerned with external trade. It also acts as arbiter. Early in 1987, several ministries and dozens of large industrial concerns were granted the right to trade directly with foreign countries. These decisions were probably wise, but it is too early to assess the benefits derived from these limited experiments.

A Litmus Test: The Private Sector

Here the new Secretary General strikes a more unusual note when he encourages the private sector, an area which had been out of bounds for his predecessors. Several criteria can be used to assess the results of economic reform in a communist country. The most significant seems to be the share of individuals in industry, agriculture and services, or rather the level of legitimacy granted to it. In reality the private sector exists anyway. It is active in all areas in which the State is inefficient. The only question is whether it remains hidden—referring to black market—or whether it is openly tolerated or even encouraged. The fact that comparatively important measures were taken toward rehabilitating the private sector explains why the reforms accomplished in two communist countries, China and Hungary, were by all accounts more effective than elsewhere.

Mikhail Gorbachev paid a great deal of attention to the matter. As early as the Party Congress in February 1986 he tackled the problem. He first concentrated on the countryside, emphasizing the advantage for the State to allow collective farms to dispose freely of their surplus produce (that is, what is left after mandatory deliveries to the State), to sell these surpluses on the *kolkhoz* market (a type of free market), or through trade cooperatives, or else to use the surpluses for other purposes, in particular to "back up private business." In other words, the agro–industrial state complex has to assist the private sector. The Secretary General continued:

> Subcontracting and work contracts will become more widely used at all levels. Brigade, group, and family will be entitled to use the means of production, including land, for a length of time determined in the contract.[22]

Behind these mild phrases looms a radical revision of the collective farm system. A redistribution of work between various "brigades" and even "families" belonging to *kolkhozes*, amounts to reintroducing the concept of family units in agriculture, discrete return to the principle of individual farming under the umbrella of collective agriculture. This seems to be the perfect formula for a campaign of decollectivization in easy stages. It is somewhat similar to what happened in China when Deng Xiaoping, without officially proclaiming the end of "People's communes," as conceived by Mao, had only to split up in communes, brigades, and teams. There was need for more caution in the USSR. Forcible collectivization in the 1930s is considered both as the biggest mistake of the Stalinist era but also as a taboo subject made all the more explosive by the fact that an entire generation of communist cadres was implicated in it. Yet the taboo has been under attack since 1987, especially after the rehabilitation of Bukharin, Stalin's chief opponent. In a report of November 2, 1987, Gorbachev himself questioned the methods of collectivization and not the principle.

In 1986 the Secretary General was not content with reforming agriculture alone. In the same report to the 27th Congress he speaks of the problem of the private sector in cooperatives. These loose associations gave considerable freedom to step in where the public sector was performing badly in areas such as services and crafts during the early days of communism. A whole range of activities was promised to such cooperatives:

> Bodies and organizations set up as cooperataives have to be more numerous in conversion work, building of dwellings, gardening associations, services, and trade.[23]

That was not all as he added in a more neutral strain:

> Proposals on regulating professions will have to be given close attention. Naurally these activities must be entirely compatible with the tenets of socialist economy, they will have to be run as collectives, or on the basis of contracts with socialist enterprises.[24]

It does not matter that Gorbachev speaks of "socialist principles," or the use of "individual" rather than "private" work. The chief point is that a wedge was gradually driven into the foundations of the regime, those taught to every schoolboy not only in the USSR but even in some Western schools: socialism abolishes private property. What still remains of it in so-called socialist countries is but the last trace of capitalism, which will gradually disappear. Ownership of the cooperative type is an inferior form compared to public ownership. *Kolkhozes*, belonging to the former type will gradually change into *sovkhozes*, etc. The least that can be said of the new doctrine is that the private sector is not only to thrive but that it is a remedy for the chronic ills of the economy.

"Individual Work"

Yet the first practical applicaiton of this new doctrine was disappointing. On November 19, 1986, the Supreme Soviet adopted a draft law on "individual work" which was supposed to introduce more flexibility, but in reality retained all the drawbacks of the old institutions. Instead of defining what was permitted or not for private enterprise, the law just listed sectors where it was tolerated. Private work was allowed in dressmaking and tailoring, hairdressing, the fur business, photography, manufacturing cooking utensils, toys and souvenirs, teaching of knitting, music, typing, translations, repairs of household machines, clothing, footwear, make–up, "if it does not involve medicine or surgery," and last but not least, "conveyance of citizens by owners of private cars." A list of forbidden activities followed: manufacturing clothing from the furs "of valuable animals shot by huntsmen," pharmacy, perfumes and cosmetics, precious stones and metals crafts, including amber; producing copying machines (agitprop services were on the look–out for trouble); teaching subjects which do not figure in official programs (the same applies here); not to mention gambling establishments, baths, games and, in plain terms, "the production of shows of any kind . . ."

The overall impression is that the new law in the hands of local authorities could be deprived of any meaning, and even be used to limit private enterprise. Thus, the inhabitants of southern regions had always offered board and lodging to "wild" tourists, that is to say those who were not sent there by their firm, to stay at "official" rest homes. According to the new law, this activity was only allowed "on the basis of contracts with individual enterprises." It is doubtful that countless private tutors were better off after the law was passed. They were now forced to make a declaration at the town hall and pay a tax on their earnings.

It seems preferable to leave private enterprise alone. Apparently Mikhail Gorbachev was also disappointed by the limits of the new law. At any rate at the June 1987 plenum he criticized its application:

> Many people wish to engage in individual paid work. It would seem that there is need for this significant development, but it meets with many delays and difficulties. The reason for this is lack of interest on the part of local authorities which do not cooperate, and sometimes even actively oppose it through bureaucratic regulations.[25]

In reality, there was a political motive behing this dragging of feet. Evoking the "ambiguous" response to the law on individual work, he waxed indignant at people debating on "not the way to make better and quicker use of the possibilities that are offered, but the legitimacy of this kind of economic activity at the present stage of socialism." Some see in cooperative and individual work a kind of reinstatement of private economy. In my opinion, comrades, from our own experience as well as that of other socialist countries, we know how useful and necessary it is to harness, within the socialist framework, such types of ecomomic activity. They help meet the basic needs of the population, drive away the "shadow economy" and all possible abuses, that is to say they restore sound social and economic relations.[24]

The reference to "shadow economy" raises the real question. It reveals the hypocrisy of fine speeches about theoretical principles. In practice private enterprise is absolutely necessary even if it is one of the "surviving features of capitalism." The extent of private enterprise was estimated by the secretary of the committee for legislative proposal on "individual work," Minister Gladki when he wrote that the "number of people engaged in individual work in general, outside agriculture" was over one hundred thousand. He hastened to add that "according to opinion surveys the figure was much higher."[27] This is very likely, especially since Gorbachev estimated the amounts of money paid by individuals to people working in the private sector to one billion and a half rubles. If the figure is correct the annual income of the 100,000 enterpreneurs would be 15,000 rubles (ten times the average salary).

So far we have dealt with the private sector aspect of the Gorbachev reforms since this is the most novel. In other respects, his economic reform is a complex and daunting task impossible to achieve. The Secretary General is a resourceful and ambitious person, as can be seen from his April 1986 appeal to the work force of the Volga automobile plant (VAZ) built by Fiat in Togliatti City:

> Every time your plant launches a new model, we are told, the new car will be equal to the best models in the world. But let me ask you a question: Why does the VAZ aspire no higher? Why should you not set yourself a better target and become the leader of fashion in the automobile industry all over the world? . . . We must give up imitating other people and following the trodden path.[28]

The VAZ factory is well known in foreign countries for producing the Lada car. However, Gorbachev's words sound unrealistic. How could its workers lead in international car design? the Secretary General cannot make the people understand the most basic truths since they have been trained to ignore them. Let us remember that the average Soviet citizen to this day knows next to nothing of payment by check, not to mention credit cards, that the ruble is a non–convertible currency and will remain so until the end of the century, that signing a mutually agreed contract between two industrial concerns, without reference to a higher authority, is unusual, that grain production is administered by the State, etc. etc.

In fact, the Secretary General is bound to act like any party leader before him, that is prefer verbal encouragements and advocate simple solutions while the population at large does not listen. If he has to rely on Soviet enterprises to find invstments in the modernization process and in order to settle the most acute social problems, achieve efficiency without increasing workers' unrest, he has a long way to go. What is, for example, the best way to reduce the enormous subsidies that the State pours into basic consumer goods? How to raise the price of meat, bread, housing, without social and political repercussions? Mikhail Gorbachev must bear in mind that such attempts brought down two party leaders in Poland. His opponents are rubbing their hands with pleasure, seeing the hazardous journey that lies ahead of him. In any event, the feeling of helplessness in economic matters led Mikhail Gorbachev to extend the economic reforms, the original *perstroika*, to politics and communications as well. Decmocratization and *glasnost*, its corollary, are henceforth seen as the key to reforms in the USSR.

Chapter VI

GLASNOST

The most striking feature of *perestroika* was its greater openness in matters of information—*glasnost*. It can even be said with perhaps only slight exaggeration that Gorbachev's original reforms are only those in culture and information media.

As a preliminary it should be pointed out that, if "transparency" is an almost accurate translation of *glasnost*, it is not to be taken literally in real life. The word (feminine gender) derives from "glas," "golos" meaning "voice" and from the verb "glasit" meaning "to make public." *Glasnost* is the noun corresponding to the latter. It is more accurate to talk of "openness," which is the word official Soviet translators use. There are also more perfidious translations of *glasnost*, such as "May I speak, sir" or "No more meaningless lies . . ."

In any event, *glasnost* has to be compared with the situation in the USSR under previous rulers if it is to be understood. It cannot be compared to conditions in the West where the most reactionary country is infinitely more "transparent" than the Soviet Union at present. The various stages of the "Irangate" affair can serve as a means of assessing the progress still to be made in Gorbachev country. It should be added that the word *glasnost* was always used in official Soviet communications even from the days of Lenin, who saw in it a way to make society more dynamic, to the infinitely more "opaque" rule of Stalin. It depends what is meant by it, and it seems that *glasnost* acquired a new meaning in two respects in the spring of 1986.

Less Taboo Subjects

At first new subjects were open to the media and to public debate. The seal of secrecy was lifted from natural and human disasters, statistical data were published, which was usually negative, such as the death rate, crime rates, alcoholism, drug addiction, incidents of divorce and various other social matters. In this context the Soviets certainly appreciate opinion polls. The phenomenon of openness is not without its political implications insofar as it is a departure from the unwritten law, in force since Stalin's days, according to which anything outside the control of the Party and leadership must be ignored by the press. The purpose of the media is primarily to educate the masses and to inform them. Obviously the USSR has never reached the peaks of Pavlovian conditioning, described by Orwell in *1984* where the "Minister of Truth" attempts to erase all words connected with undesirable or unplanned phenomena. All the same, until the last days of Brezhnev's power the rule was to ignore these phenomena since the Party, in its wisdom, saw to everything, and there was no need to inundate the readers with tales of calamities, the only exception being the Tashkent earthquake announced in 1966.

In the same vein, the use of opinion polls disproved another well established belief, that of "monolithism." Thus a population indoctrinated by this educational system, assuming less and less differences occurring between ethnic groups and social classes, reacted unexpectedly. As the results of the surveys are disclosed in "normal" figures, which are far from the 99 percent election results inherited from Stalin's agitprop and still adhered to on June 21, 1987 in local elections, the old practices will be discontinued.

In the field of communications the new policy of *glasnost* is slowly gaining ground, although not always in an atmosphere of transparency. Therefore, only later—after the April 1985 plenum—was it decided to open the question of drug addiction to the press.[1] In reality, the decision had no visible effects on the problem. At the 27th Party Congress a year later a single speaker touched on the question (the new Georgian Party chief Patiashvili), and up to the present time little is known of it.

The change became more evident after the nuclear disaster at Chernobyl in the spring of 1986. While at first a majority of the Politburo members succeded in imposing news blackout on Gorbachev, quite usual in similar accidents, the ban was lifted on May 5th, ten days after the fourth reactor had exploded. By that time the news had leaked throughout the world, along with radioactive fallout. However, information was released from then on with little censorship and contained full details in a manner unprecedented in the USSR. The direction toward *glasnost* was confirmed on other occasions during the following months. The sinking of the liner "Admiral Nakhimov" in the Black Sea, as well as other less important accidents was released immediately. In 1986 citizens who were less well off were said to have become quite worried at the sudden flood of disasters: "Since the new leadership has taken over, there have been more accidents than ever before!"

The lifting of secrecy is more significant politically when it applies to painful historical events such as collectivization or the purges of the thirties rather than when books or films banned for years are finally accessible to the public. This is what happened late in 1986 in the first part of the second stage of the Gorbachev reform. Previously when film directors and writers met at their congresses they had been given a free hand to make certain claims concerning the rehabilitation of past literary figures and subjects, such as Pasternak and ecology. Essentially political topics, such as Stalin, Khrushchev and even Brezhnev, remained out of bounds.

Starting in December 1986 things started to change in this area as well. First, there was Academician Sakharov's return to Moscow. Then the publication of Lenin's Testament appeared in the *Moscow News*, which caused a far greater stir in the general public. It was revealed that the founding father of the revolution was critical of Stalin and wished him to be "transferred to another position" from Secretary General. Still, on the eve of the momentous "January 1987 plenum," several Moscow and provincial cinemas showed "Repentance," a film made by Abuladze, a Georgian producer. It was a transparent satire of the days when Stalin and Beria were in power. A less spectacular but symbolic gesture was the opening of the Novodievich cemetery in Moscow where Khrushchev had been buried ten years earlier. Finally, starting on January 20 the BBC Russian broadcasts were no longer jammed, nor the Voice of America beginning on May 23, 1987. "Radio Liberty" in Munich, as "Number One Enemy" was still interfered with, and these measures made *glasnost* into something of an international phenomenon.

At the same time *glasnost* affected another area when, in keeping with the lifting of secrecy, additional institutions and cadres came under public scrutiny. This was not an entirely new phenomenon since in 1985, and in 1982 under Andropov, corruption had often been exploited as an instrument in the struggle for power. In this respect, *glasnost* would have been unremarkable if it had not applied to targets which so far had remained untouchable to the KGB. In December, the KGB was accused of exceeding its power in the Ukraine when the police tortured people in Karelia and interfered with ministries which had relations with foreign countries, such as the Ministry for Foreign Trade or the Defense Ministry. Some newspapers or journals specialized in such reports.

Fourteen Million New Readers

Within a few weeks the public showed enormous interest in the media. Political programs and debates on TV attracted a new audience, and the overall number of copies circulated by the Moscow press increased by fourteen million. Gorbachev was fully aware of this increased interest and explained it at great length at the January 1987 plenum:

> We need transparency, we need criticism and self criticism as
> efficient instruments of socialist democracy. More than ever
> we need to throw more light on public life so that the Party
> and the people know everything, so there remain fewer dark
> corners where mold can develop.[2]

This was not really new. Many other leaders before him had insisted on this point, and even Chernenko was said by some western diplomats stationed in Moscow to be "more open" than his colleagues because he paid lip service to democracy. This is the reason why different evidence has to be found, such as Gorbachev's explanation at the same plenum:

> Do we have proof that the process of change that is underway
> will continue to a satisfactory end, that past mistakes will
> not be repeated? The Politburo can give a positive answer to
> these questions: yes, we have evidence. . . . In the manifold
> development of democratization within the socialist regime,
> full reestablishment of Leninist principles of transparency . .
> *perestroika* is only possible through democracy and thanks
> to democracy.

Here the Secretary General strikes a more genuine chord. Not only did he go on to say, "the country must have legal guarantees to promote transparency," but a few days later he repeated in a speech to cadres of the media:

> Transparency is both the *sine qua non* condition of the de-
> mocratization process in our society, but also one of the

most important guarantees that the changes instituted are irreversible.[4]

In the space of a few months, Gorbachev managed to expose a deep-seated weakness of the system he had inherited. Until then he seemed to have been content with declarations on the "irreversibility" of *perestroika*, and its inevitability. For the first time he stressed the need to avoid falling into the same mistakes as in the past and to find guarantees to this end. To give credit where it is due he put his finger on the most efficient guarantees of democratization. It is indeed through a democratic process of change in a political system that swings between personality cult and terror, dogmatism and half-hearted reforms, in a climate of economic paralysis, corruption, and institutionalized irresponsibility, that things will be set straight.

An important landmark for *glasnost* in 1987 was the celebration of the 70th anniversary of the October Revolution, a unique opportunity for the regime to examine its history and for the leader of the Party to remove further taboos. The long-winded report Gorbachev delivered on November 2 disappointed foreign observers who had expected Trotsky's rehabilitation and other spectacular gestures. Gorbachev did not go that far but he did show unprecedented objectivity. Without using the same violent language as Khrushchev regarding Stalin, Gorbachev expressed substantially the same objections to him taking in all the stages of communism in his analysis. He considered it right to support Stalin against Trotsky and the first opposition members. He believed the policy of massive industrialization was well founded. This was no surprise since, after all, no one died of industrialization. Collectivization was another matter since it dealt with equal harshness with the middle peasants and *kulaks* and led to inexcusable excesses. Gorbachev refrained from questioning the principle but suggested, as many theoreticians before him had done, the concept that cooperatives could take other forms than *kolkhozes*.

Obviously the speech was the result of a compromise, particularly the comment on Bukharin's opposition to collectivization. The main thing, however, was that the report did not claim to be the final word on history. It was seen as a fresh stimulus for new research and more detailed studies. Furthermore, by then the Soviet press published more balanced views of the great figures of the revolution, including Trotsky. The Politburo appointed a commission to look at the question of purges. This is still a far cry from objective history when specialists will use their own judgment and not adopt a line established by political leaders. Moreover, when they are able to publish controversial writings or reassess historical events in their own way—only then will historic *glasnost* be true.

Areas of Darkness

Other significant subjects were still out of bounds for journalists. First of all, although some topics had been declassified, entire sectors remained silently banned. Military affairs were still classified, and not only was nothing known of Soviet armament programs, but it was also openly stated that Soviet casualties in Afghanistan could not be released since "the enemy would make use of the information." The same can be said of foreign policy. Nothing is ever known of Gorbachev's initiatives before they are publicly announced. Finally, the process of arriving at vital decisions in the Politburo and Secretariat is obscure. Rumors were rife during the long holidays taken by Gorbachev in the summer of 1987 and were proof of the limitation of reform. Second, *glasnost* applies mainly to some national newspapers and periodicals and is without much effect on the provincial press, which is still tightly controlled by local Party leaders. In January 1987, Gorbachev rebuked it for "lack of audacity and ideological fervor," but a few months earlier in a speech he made at Krasnodar he had been even sterner:

> During are recent plenary session of the Party Committee of the Kurgan region, first secretary Comrade Plekhanov presented a good report, which was sharp, critical, and rich in its implications. But when the report was published in the regional papers, it was pruned so much that it lost all its asperities and sounded like one last year, or even five years ago. Everything was obliterated or given the seal of approval; over thirty passages had been cut, namely those dealing with mismanagement and those containing names of people responsible for abuses or shortcomings. In short, there seem to be two levels of transparency at Kurgan: one for a restricted circle and the other for everyone else.[5]

This is not a feature of the provincial press only. Even in Moscow the most interesting analyses and revelations were to be found only in a few marginal organs. Thus, the weekly *Moscow News* was suddenly in the limelight, so that many people both in the East and the West became aware of the existence of this newssheet which had up to that time received very limited circulation. In fact, from August 1986, Egor Iakovlev, who had previously worked for *Izvestia*, became manager with the avowed intention of transforming the publication from "an information sheet for tourists to a political newspaper," because, as he explained it, "Soviet society has become politically conscious."[6] Similarly *Oganiok*, an illustrated magazine which had so far been extremely conformist, started to cause a stir in the summer of 1986 when it acquired a new editor, Vitali Korotich, a fifty-year-old Ukrainian writer. The latter explained with plenty of humor the newspaper's process of *perestroika*:

> On my arrival I found a perfectly up-to-date register instructing us how to publish a profile of such and such a person and in what format, which pamphlet of which writer and only those who enjoyed a "good" reputation had to be published before another one—whatever the quality of their work. Do you think it is easy doing away with these practices at one stroke, and then ensuring that no one feels angry with the editor?[7]

Naturally other literary journals, such as *Druzhba narodov* (Peoples' Friendship), *Znamia*, along with *Pravda* and *Izvestia* tried their best to publish new features, surveys and commentaries without losing their official character and their constraints under the established protocol. Television networks also arranged wide-ranging debates which would have been unheard of under Brezhnev. However, some daring gestures, which attracted notice abroad, after a time seemed to have limited effects. Thus, Pasternak was rehabilitated but his masterpiece, *Doctor Zhivago*, was not to be published until 1988, casting a doubt on the intentions of the authorities. As for historical "rehabilitations," most of the work was done by writers, journalists, and even poets. The official writers or historians of the Institute of Marxism-Leninism and the *Historical Questions of the CPSU* journal were much slower to change.

There is one other reservation: *glasnost* was not accompanied by far-reaching institutional changes. Nothing happened to alter the selection of newspaper editors, the mechanisms in publishing or cultural productions, which continued to remain under the Party's close ideological control, just as it did in the past. If the Party apparatus receives a new set of directives or if a few heads rolled, it would seem that *glasnost* could be revoked at any time.

The Situation Could be Reversed

In the Soviet Union in 1956, and again in 1963 and 1965, reverses did occur; they also occurred in China in December 1986 and in 1989. Moreover, reverses are recurring features of most communist countries. This feeling of *déjà vu* is by no means surprising. It reflects the dilemma facing all authoritarian regimes, *a fortiori* when they are totalitarian. Their leaders periodically realize that the system does not work, that excessive authority leads to inflated bureaucracy, sclerosis and paralysis, and that more individual freedom is needed to stimulate enterprise. But how far can the process go? When does it become risky for the system which is to be preserved and not abolished? Sooner or later the old rule has to be re–established: "You are free, as long as you act according to our wishes . . ."

Moreover, in Russia the notion of *glasnost* has always been present since educated people have a duty to introduce truth, humanity, and justice into a political system based on force and authoritarianism. As early as 1950, as Professor Gleason remarked, writer Ivan Aksakov, chief editor of *Russkaya Beseda*, made *glasnost* his favorite theme. More recently Solzhenitsyn said the same thing when he was asked about "truth": it appears more valuable to him than freedom in its institutional aspect as it is understood in the West. This is precisely the kind of *glasnost* most difficult to achieve, and for this reason Gleason believes that Gorbachev did not embark on his crusade without compelling reasons:

> Those who feel completely skeptical about Gorbachev's real intentions are probably wrong. This struggle (for *glasnost*) has been so fundamental in the history of Russia, so difficult to carry out that it has known so many Pyrrhic victories, relapses, and failures that one can hardly believe that Gorbachev enters it for the benefit of Western liberals and left–wingers alone.[8]

One of the important consequences of *glasnost* was precisely to reinstate the cultural elite's influence in national life. Just as economic paralysis had negative effects on society (alcoholism, birth rate, and corruption), so doctrinaire attitudes, hunting of dissidents, and a prevalent cynicism took their toll on intellectuals. The intelligentsia was alienated under Brezhnev, with considerable numbers emigrating, whether legally or not. While the country was losing its vital forces it was drained off its cultural resources.

The situation has improved, but one is tempted to ask whether the Secretary General did not put the cart before the horse. In the present circumstances, a policy which appeals to the intelligentsia and the media is a sign of weakness insofar as it is a desperate effort to avoid a showdown with those in power by going over the heads of the *apparatchiki*. For this reason *glasnost* must imply a reexamination of the prerogatives of the ruling apparatus if it is not to appear fragile and lacking in credibility.

Chapter VII

THE BIG CLEAN-UP

Everyone thought, especially the *apparatchiki* in Brezhnev's days, that Mikhail Gorbachev's assumption to power would lead to a complete shake-up of personnel. First of all, because stagnation (*zastoy*) of the preceding years had affected to an unprecedented degree recruitment into the upper reaches of the Party and government. The new leader admitted that the natural process of recruitment had come to a halt, so that only elderly people were left at the top. Second, because the same stagnation encouraged large-scale corruption and graft, which are a permanent feature of authoritarian or totalitarian regimes, that purges had to follow. Even before reaching power Andropov launched an anti-corruption campaign to defeat the Brezhnev group. Gorbachev and his team were bound to follow in his footsteps.

Gerontocracy

The scene of shuffling old men twice a year climbing with difficulty the steps of Lenin's mausoleum for official parades was unedifying. However, this sorry picture of gerontocracy gave only a faint picture of the size of the problem: not only was the Politburo's average age over seventy but the entire apparatus was also out of date.

In 1981, the last congress of the Brezhnev era demonstrated stagnation most conclusively as the proportion of old Central Committee members retaining their seats was over 90 percent. It was much higher in reality since one-fifth of the missing members had died since the previous congress. Those under fifty years of age amounted to 7.5 percent, 53 percent were over sixty, and 16 percent were over seventy. It should be remembered that all governing bodies (Secretariat and Politburo) had been re-elected without any changes. This had never happened at any other congress in the entire history of the Soviet CP.

In the government and Soviet hierarchy, old age was the rule in the spring of 1984, the "new" government was a reflection of the old. It made the USSR a confirmed world champion in gerontocracy—the only "challenger" could have been the Vietnamese government in another communist country. Out of 101 members of the Council of Ministers, 46, nearly half, were over the retirement age of sixty–five, and 29 were over seventy. As for those less than fifty years old, there were a total of 3, all appointed since Brezhnev's death. Gerontocracy was also the norm in all other sectors. Thus, in scientific research, doctoral candidates under forty years of age amounted to only 10 percent in 1986, while ten years earlier the rate was 29 percent. The average age for completing a thesis was forty–eight in science, but it was fifty–two in social sciences, a hunting ground for ideologists and the old guard.[1] The situation was the same in culture, also the preserve of powerful cliques. The result was that at the Writers' Union Congress, although it took place a year after Gorbachev had assumed power, among the 567 delegates, 99 were in their seventies and eighties, with only 15 delegates under forty and 3 under thirty–five.[2] Furthermore, as it was pointed out by a delegate, two of the three "kids" were—as luck would have it—from the small Baltic republic of Latvia.

Corruption

As for the struggle against corruption, it was a highly topical question, but Gorbachev was only following in Andropov's footsteps. Even Chernenko made attempts at stamping it out. A significant example can be found in Uzbekistan, after Sharaf Rashidov, the local potentate died in 1983. He died at the age of seventy–six after leading the Party for over a quarter of a century. In this Central Asian republic Rashidov was omnipotent. He was an important dignitary in Tashkent in Stalin's days (chairman of the local Writers' Union in 1949, President of the Uzbek Republic in 1950). He was also one of the oldest candidate members of the Politburo, since 1961, and a close friend of Brezhnev. On October 31, 1983 it was announced that Rashidov had died "suddenly." In reality, he had probably committed suicide to avoid the consequences of the "cotton scandal" in Uzbekistan. It was alleged in the press that cotton statistics were systematically inflated to "give an illusory impression of prosperity." Inversely they could have been artificially low to allow Rashidov and his associates to sell surpluses on the black market, as others claimed.[3] One thing is certain, figures were shamefully distorted and it took a long time for the scandal to come out into the open. Thus, on December 23 1983, almost three months after Rashidov's death, the Central Committee approved a government decree to "perpetuate Rashidov's memory" as had been done with Brezhnev. His character was unsullied.

Only much later, in June 1984, did the skeleton come out of the closet to be seen by a small circle on "the intervention and close assistance of the Central Committee of the CPSU."[4] In other words Moscow had to order an investigation. The results were made public only in February 1986, and it was not until the following June that the decree of December 23, 1983 was revoked and Rashidov's cult buried.[5] Heads began to roll. Rashidov's successor, Usmankhodzhaev, stated in his report that half the *nomenklatura* of the republican Central Committee and of the regional committees had been replaced.[6] Specifically, 10 out of 11 regional first secretaries were fired over a period of eighteen months; 200 deputies of the local Soviets, most of which had been elected in 1985, were dismissed. In August 1986, Usmanov, minister of cotton growing, was sentenced to death by the USSR Supreme Court. All 14 members of his ministry's "college" were prosecuted for false evidence and bribery.[7] Other death sentences followed when Karimov, first secretary of the Samarkand region, was condemned in June 1987[8]

Another typical example of corruption was in Moscow City where more details of the anti–corruption operation became known after the energetic action and outspoken comments of Boris Yeltsin. He was sent to Moscow to lead the Party and clean it up in December 1985, and he was purged less than two years later. Already under his predecessor, Grishin, 86 industrial managers and bureaucrats had been expelled from the Party for misappropriation of funds.[9] Under Yeltsin the figure rose to 20,000 Party members expelled; 30,000 excessive research assistants were sent back to work in factories, and finally 800 commercial agents were arrested. Yet it was only a beginning since the Grand Inquisitor Yeltsin declared: "We dig further and further down but can never find the bottom of this cesspool."[10]

In Kazakhstan, Kunaev, Brezhnev's companion and Politburo member, did not fall until December 1986. However, in February 1986 he was criticized for "having necessarily been aware" of the misdemeanors of two regional secretaries who had been dismissed a year earlier. Along with them 500 high civil servants had been fired.[11]

The same anti–corruption operation brought down many a Brezhnevite elsewhere. At Dnepropetrovsk, birthplace of the old Secretary General, the first secretary fell in April 1987, but between January 1985 and September 1986 "19 leading communists of the Obkom *nomenklatura* were deprived of their offices because of incompetence or undesirable associations."[12] In September 1986, 44 leaders were found guilty by courts of justice in the town of Krivoi Rog in the same region where 79 cases of forgery and falsification of accounts also came under investigation.[13] In Moldavia, another of Brezhnev's strongholds, proceedings were still going on in 1989. Fifty leaders were demoted in 1984 and 1985 for "immoderate style of living, extravagant spending and abuse of power for self–interest."[14] The head of the local party, Simeon Grossu, was reprimanded in October 1986 for "serious shortcomings in the application of Party instructions for the eradication of the practice of forgery."[15] However, he was still in power in November 1987.

The total numbers of corruption cases are difficult to estimate. In March 1987, State Prosecutor Rekunkov, announced that in the year 1986 alone and for the USSR as a whole 200,000 civil servants were given administrative punishment, and 32,000 had to pay fines.[16] What is the value of these official figures since the cases of the *nomenklatura* are not known?

From fragmentary evidence released in the press covering mostly the 1985–86 period, it seems that the proportion of cadres who lost their privileges varies between 10 and 30 percent according to the region, with peaks in Central Asia and Moscow.

Inequalities in Recruiting

This hidden purge (the word used is "purification") goes hand in hand with the normal renewal of cadres due to retirements or deaths. Job changes are a "softer" type of purges in the administrative bodies where major shifts took place. Surveys of the highest appointments show the rate of replacement in all Party institutions as higher than under any previous new Secretary General—for example, Stalin in the fifties and Khrushchev in the sixties. This is most noticeable in the Politburo and Secretariat, but much less so in the Central Committee where the difference, especially compared to the changes under Stalin, is quite unimportant.

Of course the changes that a new Secretary General can effect in the Central Committee in the first years of his mandate are necessarily modest. This rule stands out clearly where rates of replacement and reelection of the old members in the various Central Committees since Lenin's death are compared. With the exception of two congresses held in 1939 under unusual circumstances, after the apparatus had been decimated by the great purge and then in 1952 thirteen years later, they all show remarkable continuity: between 25 percent and 10 percent new members at each congress; between 60 percent and 80 percent of old members re-elected, but with a higher rate of replacement during the second congress of each ruler. In 1961, Khrushchev was politically stronger than in 1956, hence bringing in over 63 percent new members, many more than at his first congress. Similarly Brezhznev could place many more friends in 1971, with 38 percent new members, than in 1966 with 29 percent. From then on, Brezhnev increased the Central Committee systematically and added new friends without discarding old ones. Gorbachev gave up the practice, which means that both the number of old members and new were reduced.

In the first stage, at any rate, no major upheaval occurred. First of all, the replacement of cadres was not accompanied by institutional changes, either in the Party or in its working. Thus an analysis of the membership of the new Central Committee confirmed the remarkable stability of power in the main branches of the Party apparatus, from Brezhnev to Gorbachev. Men may have changed more than in the past, but the relative power of their functions were the same. In other words, the seats in the parliament of the Party go to the same regional *apparatchiki* (the strongest group with over a fourth of full members), government members, etc., followed by the military, diplomats, security men—all in the same order of precedence and in same proportions. Another disappointment is in store. It was hoped that with modernization and rationalization, university professors and academicians would enter this elitist preserve. Nothing of the sort happened. There were two more academicians in Brezhnev's Central Committee than in Gorbachev's. The share of graduates went down from 20 percent to 17 percent. It should be pointed out that Gorbachev's pleas for modifying the rules governing the recruitment of cadres had remained so far without significant effect. In January 1987, the Secretary General caused something of a stir in his report to the plenum. He suggested the general application of a principle that had been tried out in the Baltic Republics which made industrial managers and technical personnel (up to foremen and brigade leaders) subject to elections. Concerning the election of deputies to

the Soviets, he was slightly more prudent and hid behind proposals
supposedly sent to him by rank and file:

> Most proposals suggested having several candidates at elec-
> tions and at pre–electoral selection meetings. It was also
> deemed desirable that elections be held in larger constituen-
> cies, which would return several deputies each. Our com-
> rades think this would allow each citizen to express his opin-
> ion to a wider panel of candidates, as well as give party or-
> ganizations and Soviets a chance to be better informed of
> the need and aspirations of the population.[17]

To an inexperienced mind this might sound like an invitation to
a multi–party political system, but it is nothing of the kind. Not
only because Mikhail Gorbachev, just as all other communist leaders,
thinks that the Party has to keep overall control, but also because,
even in the existing situation of a "communist and non–party bloc,"
the principle of several candidates for one seat was never ratified.
It rather means that in Gorbachev's mind the democratic process is
intensified with an increase in the size of constituencies, i.e., there
will be more candidates for more seats. From a one–man poll to
changes in candidate numbers this appears as progress. However,
a new emphasis is laid on "electoral assemblies" and "preelectoral
conferences," and what happens in the voting booth, and the choice
facing the elector seems less important. In accordance with an old
communist tradition, the message is that real democracy does not
mean secret ballot, the last stage of a truly "democratic" process
that goes a long way back involving meetings and "contradictory "
debates. The voting bulletin loses its significance in favor of electoral
assemblies, which ensures that the Party, the sole organizer of the
debates, cannot lose.

Secret Ballot in the Party: A Small Dent in the System

Even in this light, Gorbachev's proposals were a good start, especially if accompanied with elections inside the Party. The Secretary
General had to tread even more softly:

> We have to envisage a change in the electoral procedure for
> electing committee secretaries at borough, town, region, and
> territory levels and to control committees of the federated
> republics. It has been suggested by some comrades that
> secretaries, including first secretaries, should be elected by

secret ballot at corresponding plenums of Party Committees. Party Committee members would be entitled to enter any number of candidates on the list.[18]

Naturally, Gorbachev used as a safeguard the "irreversible principle" according to which "the highest institutions in the Party have to confirm all decisions taken by committees which are below them, even appointments of cadres." In other words, elections, although free and secret, would not be valid until they had been ratified at the top. However, this was an important improvement, especially when compared to communist parties abroad. Everywhere large assemblies (consisting of all members of congresses or regional conferences) elected in a "secret ballot" an executive committee (regional committee or central committee) usually by dropping in the ballot box a list of candidates prepared by the organizers. So far such committees served as parliaments during the lengthy period of five years between two congresses. In turn they held elections at their first meetings, but with raised hands this time; thus political bureau (Politburo) and secretariat, including the number one Secretary General, were not really elected.

If it is noted that the present norm is for the latter to become the "Supreme Leader" and later the "Guide," it should also be remembered that the supreme body, whether collective or not, has the last say in everyone's career, starting with those of its own electors, the Central Committee's members. It is by no means a trivial matter to know the conditions and the way each of them votes. This explains why the system of voting with raised hand has been an important element—though not the only one—of the system of "democratic centralism" which has changed the election of Party managers into a process of mutual cooperation, resulting in a personal dictatorship, or "fossilization" and gerontocracy. Thus, Gorbachev's idea to elect regional secretaries by secret ballot and to allow voting on "any number of candidates" is an important dent in the system of democratic centralism.

A more drastic measure suggested by Khrushchev in 1961 was the restriction of elective mandates. The one sure way of preventing "local bosses" from hanging onto their positions and exerting discretionary power for life is to force them to retire after four, six, or eight years in power. In 1961, only small numbers of replacements had been allowed for each election (for example, one–fourth for the Politburo and Central Committee). What happened to these measures is well known, although they had been approved by the Congress and entered into Party statutes.

The Plenum Disapproved

In January 1987, Mikhail Gorbachev was still far from the relative success that had been achieved by his predecessor Khrushchev a quarter of a century earlier. Not only were his proposals more limited but they were not endorsed by the Central Committee. In its final resolution the principle of elections in industry were approved, and elections to the Soviets were more or less endorsed so long as they followed the communist tradition, which made electoral assemblies more important than voting booths. As for elections for Party offices, the Central Committee refused the principle of secret ballot and all the other amendments that Gorbachev proposed. The wording of the resolution, no less complicated than ambiguous is a gem:

> The plenum is in agreement with the Politburo's motion on the principle of the need to increase democracy within Party ranks in order to search for the best ways to improve the work of grass root organizations, conferences, and plenums, and to perfect the mechanism of appointing elected Party organs at every level, in the area of democratization . . .[19]

A few experiments in elections involving several candidates were attempted even before official authorization had been given. This indicates, if not a progression toward a rule of law, the tenacity of the Secretary General and his resourcefulness. Thus, in the elections of local Soviets, which took place on June 21, 1987, 93 constituencies broke the regulations and allowed several contestants—about 200 in all.[20] This figure contrasted sharply with a total of 2,321,766 local deputies elected on the same day. Slightly more significant, in view of the negative attitude of the CC plenum, was a "contested" election a few days later at a *raikom* (a rural borough) in the Komorovo region. There were two candidates, Ivan Malkov, chairman of the borough executive committee (*raispolkom*, the equivalent of *raikom*, but in the local government) and his deputy Guennadi Sedykh. The contested election was the idea of Yermakov, the first regional secretary. He also kept a close watch on the proceedings but was not entirely satisfied with the results. *Soviet Russia* reported the election as follows:

> The electoral campaign was a clash of personalities, not a discussion of each candidate's electoral platform, as Yer-

makov wished. Praises were heaped, first on Ivan Malkov's capacity to correct his worst faults, then on Sedykh's open mind, to such an extent that Zagorulko, head of the local *sovkhoz*, pointed out that it was essential for electors to follow the Party line rather than their feelings for a particular person. Malkov was elected by 29 votes against 20, but Sedykh was not out yet. Yermakov decided that he would remain in reserve for another election.[21]

The Nomenklatura and Its Privileges

Was Mikhail Gorbachev going to lay his hands on the other aspect of the Leninist–Stalinist system, that is material privileges enjoyed by its dignitaries? It is common knowledge that from the times of war communism under Lenin the Party has allowed officials preferential treatment, which in times of economic shortages and even famine was of considerable importance. Thus, special stores offer such officials better goods than in the state shops, while holiday vouchers give them access to luxury hotels, chauffeur–driven cars, and a range of special "canteens." All these advantages are enjoyed by Party officials according to a meticulous pecking order. They are far removed from the egalitarian concepts of the October Revolution, and they ensure obedience at all levels. Stalin killed only irreducible leaders but had others toe his line through this system of privileges untouched by his successors. "Good–bye dacha, Party store, cars," said the official who had been dismissed, and each career set back also means an appreciable lowering of services. In a country where access to small luxuries is impossible, these in–built privileges are priceless, especially to those at the receiving end.

The legitimacy of these advantages came under scrutiny in the early stages of Gorbachev's *perestroika*. It must be admitted that no change has occurred so far in this area since the Secretary General proves much more timid than others have. It was not until before the 27th Congress that the subject of special stores was raised in "Letters from Party Members" cleverly tampered with by *Pravda*. Millions of readers were dumbfounded when they read an excerpt from a letter signed by one Mikolaev, "Party member since 1940," from Kazan:

> On the subject of social justice, one cannot ignore the fact that Party leaders, the Soviets, trade unions, the economy, or the Komsomol by using all kinds of special restaurants,

shops, hospitals, etc., increase social inequality. Yes we are a socialist country; let it be so, without insisting on egalitarianiam—the leaders must receive a higher pay. In other respects there should be no privileges. The boss can shop in the normal places and queue up like everyone else. This may be a way to put an end to those endless queues which we are all sick of.[27]

It reflected the thoughts of many people, but it also frightened thousands of *nomenklatura* members who started counteraction. Speakers at the congress referred to the article in no uncertain terms. One of them, Yegor Ligachev, second–in–command in the Party, openly criticized the newspaper for its slip–up without specifying what he had in mind. The only person who dared to touch the taboo was Yeltsin, the new Moscow Party chief. He did not directly question privileges, but attacked "private goods," in other words, advantages people in power enjoy:

In my opinion, where benefits enjoyed by leaders at all levels are not justified, they have to be cancelled. This will bring about increased dynamism in the work force and society at large, and our ideological opponents will be deprived of powerful arguments.[23]

At the time Yeltsin was regarded as Gorbachev's spokesman on many subjects, so it is likely that this latest message had been approved by the Secretary General. Another sign was that neither *Pravda*'s board nor the person who concocted the letter, a journalist named Samelia, were punished, in spite of Ligachev's indignation. Chief editor Afanasiev confirmed the point in person in October 1986, adding that "apart from a few stylistic details that needed improvement," he was in agreement with the publication of the letter. About the same time the editorial board of *Kommunist*, the ideological journal of the Party, allowed an economist, Tatyana Zaslavskaya, to write on the same subject more analytically and draw conclusions relevant to the the economy in general:

The fact that various sectors of the community are unable to gain access to a certain category of retail shops gives rise to a specific form of social inequality and in practice leads to several consumers' markets coexisting, with varying rates for the purchasing power of the ruble.[24]

Yeltsin's fall in November 1987 undoubtedly struck a heavy blow to any hopes that privileges might become less obstructive. The Moscow Party leader was quietly detested by his peers—not only in the capital but in other regions—for closing the special department stores of the City Party committee on Kirov Street. *Apparatchiki* everywhere sighed with relief when he was dismissed.

If we admit that Gorbachev allowed the debate on this difficult question to develop, it is also obvious that he did his best to stop it. He made two statements about it, one in a speech to a Russian audience, addressing Soviet media officials, the other addressing a group of foreigners in an interview to *Unita*. In both cases he did not show much enthusiasm for abolishing the privileges of the Soviet *nomenklatura*. The first such speech revealed that he had no intention of implementing reforms in this area. He did not refer to the special stores accessible only to Party dignitaries, but to canteens and sanatoria attached to factories. Pretending to believe that critics of privileges were mostly incensed by those, he declared:

> Are we to stop from encouraging a writer, a talented scientist, or any other honest and industrious person? Are we to hold up the flag of the bourgeois concept of social justice and abolish pensions, sanatoria and rest homes belonging to large industrial concerns? This would be yielding to petty thinking and our attempt to fight inequality would make us guilty of a far greater kind of social injustice. Comrades, this must become clear—social justice does not mean leveling.[25]

While talking to *Unita* journalists, Gorbachev was a little more honest and mentioned the existence of special stores in industry as well as for the Writers' Union and the Academy of Science, and even "those accessible to the Party apparatus," but they were a "relic of the past." He also confessed:

> Of course, such a system can create problems. Excesses do occur, and some are too far removed from the living conditions of ordinary people. Such cases naturally give rise to justified criticisms on the part of workers.[26]

Thus, although the existing situation was unfair, the system itself was not at risk. It was sufficient to put certain "excesses" right. There was no possibility of an "August 4" operation for abolishing *nomenklatura* privileges.

The "Stagnant" Category

Higher turnover among cadres of many institutions did not change the fact that many remained, or "stagnated." In spite of Gorbachev's changes they retained the positions they held under Brezhnev. The "rate of stagnation" appears to be at its highest in the Central Committee where 56.5 percent full members were there already in October 1982, with first regional secretaries holding out longest. Nearly 55 percent of them were in office before Gorbachev, just over one-third were in under Brezhnev and seventeen of them, 11 percent, were in the same job ten years earlier.

Naturally this proportion varies considerably in each republic. It is the highest in places where the first secretary is also a "figure of the past": Baltic Republics, Moldavia, and above all the Ukraine, where Shcherbitsky's prolonged presence prevented any upheaval. This applies to the years before 1987. Early that year things began to change in the Ukraine as well with high officials replaced, such as the chairman of the local KGB, the head of local government, etc.

In any event, Shcherbitsky became both the most ancient Politburo member and one of the oldest secretaries of a large region or republic after the fall of Grishin and Kunaev from their corresponding Moscow and Kazakhstan jobs. His fall was inevitable since he was approaching seventy. Yet his amazing power of survival is probably not due to enduring the "sclerosis of the Brezhnev type" alone. The Ukraine is not Kazakstan and its first secretary is not corrupt and mediocre like Kunaev. It was revealed after the Chernobyl catastrophe in 1986 that Shcherbitsky was one of the few officials to draw the Politburo's attention to the risks involved in building a powerful nuclear station near Kiev. While in Moscow Ligachev, rather than Gorbachev, tried to promote Russian nationalism, and under cover of the "cadre mobility" sent Russian officials to replace "national" ones. Such actions by Moscow merely led to the closing of ranks behind Shcherbitsky, a Ukrainian. The riots at Alma-Ata too indicate strong resentments as seen when Kolbin, a Russian, was appointed to lead the Kazakhstan Party. There was a lesson for Gorbachev to be more prudent.

New Blood: Mature People

As for the age of those who were promoted under Gorbachev, one should discard a notion widely held in the West which believes that the new recruits were all "young Turks" impatient to replace the older generation, that is men in their forties who take over from those in their seventies. In reality, the difference in age was not that great.

To gain a better picture, the average age of people can be compared in the Gorbachev era with the age of the men who were being replaced— not at the present day but when they were appointed twenty years ago. It appears that the new team led by "young Gorbachev" was definitely older than that assembled by "old Brezhnev." Out of forty identical jobs, one-third of new appointees are over sixty, while there were only 5 percent twenty years ago; only 16 percent are under fifty, against 35 percent in the intake of 1965-66. The same applies to the Central Committee, only three of the full members elected in 1966 were over sixty years old; in 1986 twenty-one people in their sixties and two in their seventies were included among the new ones. Those over seventy make up 10 percent of the total number, which is less than in the last Central Committee under Brezhnev in 1981 (nearly 17 percent) but still significant.

It should also be remembered that Gorbachev is one of the full members of the Politburo of longest standing, and at the age of fifty-six, the youngest. This is not likely to change in the near future since none of the twenty-one new figures appointed since 1985, either in the Politburo or the Secretariat, was under fifty in 1987, compared to nine who were over sixty. As it has been noted earlier, the Secretary General likes to have older people around in order to seek their advice. Another reason is that immobilism in the highest echelons under Brezhnev has led to intermediate leaders being exceptionally old. In the 1960s and 1970s "juniors" had to bide their time longer than they normally do in the capacity of deputies or vice ministers. Since they make up the recruitment pool for the new leaders their age is inevitably mature.

Chapter VIII

THE OPPOSITION

It is impossible to reform the Soviet system or Soviet society without encountering strong resistance. In order to review these reforms, it should be said that the Soviet regime is the most conservative on earth. It is no exaggeration to call the reactions to Gorbachev's reforms an active opposition. It is situated in three sectors:

The apparatus. The whole system grew up immune from outside pressures, unlike most other political systems which had to evolve under pressure. On the contrary it is used to withstanding pressure as fiercely as possible. In fact the whole world could collapse around the *apparatchiki* and they would stick to their ways of thinking and go on acting as before, carrying on with propaganda and haranguing the crowds. This is exactly the reaction, although it has no bearing on reality. It is obvious that the train of reforms started by Gorbachev must have been a course of anxiety. As he showed his intentions more and more clearly, the opposition became more determined. Together with the apparatus, several factions are resisting reforms. They are those who have built administrative empires for themselves, as individuals or as groups. Under Stalin "socialist realism" was identical to Marxism–Leninism. Therefore, the only permissible form of creativity had to be based on dogma; although this imperative was not stated in the writings of the founding fathers, it was officially by Stalin. However, the dogma was upheld silently by succeeding generations and Soviet culture fossilized under the yoke of the so–called "creative unions" enforcing on all and sundry the most conservative writers and artists.

These "creators," who are usually unremarkable but enjoy official recognition, were in the vanguard of the fight against Khrushchev's reforms, and now they resist Gorbachev's reforms as their monopoly and privileges are in jeopardy. As literature traditionally is a vehicle for dissent (in Russia it has always been the preserve of veiled political opposition), a gang of conservative and Stalinist writers are very vocal in expressing the secret thoughts of the opposition inside the Party apparatus. The recurrent themes of their complaints are the need to praise the "heroic days" of socialism (not only the war, but also collectivization), to glorify the old generation, to fight "ideological subversion carried out by imperialism," and to refrain from making unpatriotic revelations.

With the population at large Gorbachev's new philosophy of altering old habits, which have affected a large section of the population, including the those in the circle of the apparatus, is not popular since the old system has its advantages-for many. "I pretend to work, you pretend to pay me" was the saying. In other words, although wages are low, at least everyone gets paid and without much effort. It is enough to clock in and to keep quiet, never showing any individuality or initiative, since this would only get you into trouble. Goods are few in the shops, but through an illegal network you have access to a few luxuries—much less than your boss, but maybe more than your neighbor who joined a less efficient "circuit."

According to a well-known tale, a Soviet Jew was given a sum of money by the government after emigrating to Israel, as well as a place to live and a shop, but he did not feel satisfied since the government forgot to provide customers and his shop was empty. Whether the story is true or not, it shows a mentality which explains why any reform involving a return to individual responsibility will have trouble taking root. Contrary to common belief, a large majority of Soviet industralists are not in favor of a free market system which would be open to competition. They much prefer the present bureaucratic system relying on political support for advancement and privileges, while failures can always be blamed on "objective conditions" or someone higher up. Even a shop assistant is better off receiving his employer's handouts and making private deals because of his job than giving customers good service, both more tiring and useless anyway due to the shortage of goods.

All these groups are combined in opposition to Gorbachev's policy. It is remarkable that the opposition movement is officially acknowledged, a departure from past practices. Khrushchev was met with fierce opposition also, but it was not admitted until his defeat in 1957. Before that time, although there were strong suspicions,

there was no proof Stalin's cult was discontinued. Improved relations
with Tito, offensive to old–timers like Molotov or Voroshilov, were
kept in the background. The only example of similar opposition goes
back to the 1920s. Then the struggle with the intra–party opposition
was made public. Stalin and his henchmen used it to frighten the
people. Nowadays the situation is rather similar but the opposition
remains faceless. Thus, even *glasnost* does not lead to open political
struggle. However, it was denounced by Gorbachev at the 27th Party
Congress in March 1986. He realized then how powerful the opposition was, and his admonishments were received with an expression of
incredulity. He confided his disappointment to Togliatti workers in
April 1986:

> Today mere verbal declarations in support of Party decisions
> are not good enough. . . . If someone thinks that the
> congress is over, criticisms have been vented and everything
> is well, I have to reply that changes have to be made.[1]

In June 1986, he sounded more severe: "In many places everything is as before. Any initiative meets with utter indifference, when
it is not open hostility."[2] He spoke out then at the Party Central
Committee, but when talking to writers a few days later he became
more aggressive toward "drunkards, profiteers, squanderers of public money, and bureaucrats who cling to their privileges." Even more
concretely he attacked the Gosplan all–powerful State Planning Committee:

> These officials do not respect anybody, not even the Central
> Committee and the Secretary General. They do what they
> want, and what they enjoy most of all is for people to come
> begging in their offices.[4]

In the same address he spoke about managers:

> Industrial managers write to us saying: "We have no need of
> new rights and independence. Let everything be as it is. We
> can do our work more easily." They cannot and they will
> not. A new generation has to take over before *perestroika*
> can have an effect.

From autumn 1986 opposition to Gorbachev seems to have increased, and its shape became fuller and more precise. Gorbachev,
probably in an attempt to divide the opponents, made a distinction
between two kinds of opposition—one which is good and the other

bad. On September 18, he made a speech in Krasnodar where he described the bad one as people who:

> are mostly concerned with preserving the old order, to keep their privileges. . . . We can see them today gesticulating in support of *perestroika*, making more noise than anyone else, but in reality they hinder its application under all sorts of pretexts, even the most noble ones. Let everyone hear my warning: workers know about them and retribution will come. Today some will be punished, tomorrow others. Let me remind the audience of this in case some people had forgotten it.[4]

As we can see, some opponents used "noble" pretexts to oppose him and they felt they deserved better treatment:

> Some people have sent letters to the Party Central Committee (I have them with me) saying: "We are all in favor of *perestroika*, but there are too many criticisms about it." Is everything wrong in our country? Some say we have to continue to criticize but also show the positive side of *perestroika*. I could support such a resolution.[5]

At another occasion, on April 16, 1987, he told the congress of communist youth (Komsomol):

> There is an ongoing debate as to whether we are not overdoing criticism, whether such wide-ranging *glasnost* (transparency) is necessary, and whether democracy will not lead to chaos. This debate does not seem negative to us, as it reflects in its own way a wish for social stability.[6]

At the other extreme are those who blow the process out of proportion, "who do not see in restructuring what it is, but like to rock the boat, prefering a complete renunciation of our principles."[7] This was said evidently in response to dogmatic minds who accused Gorbachev of betraying the cause of communism. If they cannot be silenced together with the opposition it is not so much that they act in good faith but that they are too powerful. Their turn will also come "later," as it has been seen before. In the meantime, Gorbachev can only invoke against them a famous precedent of 1920:

> It was the same at the time of the NEP (the new economic policy) launched by Lenin after the civil war, which called on private enterprise, when Lenin had a great deal of trouble

impressing upon people the need for a new economic policy
and demonstrating that it was not a return to capitalism
but a prerequisite for the building of socialism.[8]

Of course, if we examine the speeches of people who were under
less constraint than Gorbachev and who had embraced the new policy
enthusiastically, we find them more outspoken. So it is with Vitali
Korotich, the "liberal" chief editor of *Ogoniok*:

In my opinion, we can distinguish more and more clearly a
group of people for whom opposition to *perestroika* is a condition of survival. They are ready for anything, as was seen
in some Central Asian republics [a reference to the Alma-
Ata riots believed to have been organized by associates of
Kunaev, the fallen Kazakhstan leader]. How sad that some
individuals refuse to see the truth.[9]

But even more serious, Korotich found himself under threat:

Lately I have been repeatedly warned against provoking Soviet authorities too much. . . . People of various ages
and rank shake their heads at you, sadly saying, "Don't get
excited, we haven't seen anything yet. The day will come
when you will have to give accounts. Don't be rash."[10]

Another writer who had committed himself to the new policies,
Alexander Bovin, also alluded to those who today "keep quiet" but
who "are still hoping that their time will come." They count on a
new generation of officials "more modern in manner, but still imbued
with concepts of the past decades." He is full of ill forebodings when
he stated:

My friends, try to reassure me, don't worry, you overestimate
the power of former leaders. It will all end well. But I am
not convinced, especially since I remember that twice before
they pushed us back, they blocked the way to changes which
were absolutely necessary.[11]

Bovin alluded there to the expectations after the 20th congress which
were disappointing, and to the short burst of liberalization following
Khrushchev's fall. In reality, the present day opposition is very similar
to the old and uses the same arguments.

However, the most vocal of the new men proved to be Gorbachev
himself, who exclaimed in the middle of the full–blown political crisis,
which was to result in the downfall of his associate Boris Yeltsin in
November 1987:

We cannot ignore the opposition of conservative forces which sees in *perestroika* a threat to their own interests and selfish objectives. . . . There are quite a number of difficulties and contradictions, sometimes coming from unexpected quarters. . . . There appears to be some uncertainty and indecision about it. . . . Some people, even now, prefer to point out mistakes rather than remedy shortcomings. Nobody, of course, comes out openly against *perestroika*. No, they complain about negative effects (*izderjki*), and they invoke ideological principles claiming they will be under threat because of increasing capacity for action of the masses. How long shall we be frustrated in our policy by the ghost of these ill effects? Some are unavoidable, yes, especially in a new context. But immobilism, stagnation, and indifference are much more perverse in their consequences and costly than the effect of the process of creating new forms of social intercourse.[12]

There are some familiar arguments quoted in Gorbachev's rebuttal, and the worst error lies in the fear of "erring." "Changes cannot occur without any cost." Now let us see who are the men who use these arguments. Gorbachev whetted the public's appetite when he declared at the Komsomol congress in April 1987:

Sometimes the questions are asked: Has *perestroika* met with opposition? From which quarters? I even receive letters begging: "Mikhail Sergeyevich, give us a few names at least." I think the time has come to throw some light on the matter.[13]

Unfortunately for his audience the Secretary General stopped short, merely saying: "We have no political opponents at home." All the same, some culprits can easily be found in the world of culture, where—as was said above—people define their personal positions more readily.

The Russian Writers' Faction

Preventive action was taken by writers after the great "leap forward" provoked by Gorbachev's policies in December 1986 and January 1987. In Moscow on March 17, a meeting was held of the secretariat of the Writers' Union of the Russian Federation, a body traditionally more conservativae than the Writers' Union of the USSR.[14] The minutes, published in the union's weekly did not directly criticize

the Secretary General but gave an idea of the orgy of recriminations
aired against his reforms.

The note was struck early on by the union's first secretary, so-
called author of the Soviet anthem, father and guarantor of the cultural *nomenklatura* of the Stalin–Brezhnev era, Sergei Mikhalkov.
But even he proved less extreme in his criticism than the rank and
file contenting himself with expressing a feeling of sadness:

> Criticism is sometimes so sharp that the press is full of of-
> fensive words toward people who worked hard for the Soviet
> Union. . . . Today, many people are willing to ignore those
> with decorations, Peoples' Artists of the USSR, etc. This
> is a worrisome development, comrades. Behind the slogans:
> "Long live *glasnost*, long live *perestroika!*" speculators, un-
> talented persons, and sinister individuals are lurking in the
> shadows.

The floodgates opened thereafter. First the writer Proskurin was
attacked, then came attacks on newspapers, the fashionable weekly
Moscow News, and the journalists were denounced for trading in
"provocation," "hooliganism" and "gutter style." *Ogoniok* which dis-
plays "esoteric tendencies" and "caste outlook which had disappeared
in our country in the 1920s." Even *Pravda* received more than its
share:

> Several generations of young peopole ready to devote their
> lives to literature are ashamed to use the term "communist"
> in their writings. But our critics keep quiet. *Pravda* and
> *Literaturnaya Gazeta* discusses the latest novel published in
> Argentina. Yet what happens on our doorstep in Russia
> is not worth its notice. Has the word "communist" been
> banned, does it exist in our lives? Several generations of
> young writers seem to be ashamed of it. This must be at
> the center of our debate.

Another speaker, M. Alexeyev, gave no name but waxed indignant all the same:

> Alas, *glasnost* in literature is used by the very people who
> were always demagogues at heart. Today these "tributes
> of Truth" benefit from the use of powerful loudspeakers.
> . . They consider themselves as sole repositories of Truth.
> Many reason in this way, and if not today, when? They take

advantage of the present mood to square old scores with everyone.

Evidently they did not dare to openly condemn the reform measures that had official backing from the Party, but used endless discussions to limit them. Thus, A. Keshokov thinks that if Pasternak's *Doctor Zhivago* is to be published, it should not appear in a journal such as *Novy Mir* or other periodicals with a wide readership, because it would cause "an unnecessary stir"; it is better to publish it as a book in a limited edition. Before this intervention another writer, Dementiev, had expressed regrets that Nabokov's rather mediocre poems had been enthusiastically acclaimed. According to Shuev, this publication was not a bad thing, but it should have been accompanied by a "good commentary," as was the case with Pasternak's work. He did not think it right either to praise these rehabilitated authors to the skies "as if no others had ever-existed."

Already in the 1960s the debate between "fathers and sons" had overshadowed the underlying conflict between Stalinists and the others, which had never reached a conclusion. Today fathers have turned into grandfathers but they remember everything and become even more agitated in the face of their grandchildren's attitudes. Thus one Alexeyev cried:

> The young, the young, the young! We were also young once. Before the war my generation was prepared for the war that fascism forced upon us. If art and literature had not given us a moral backbone, we would have perished. We were cold, hungry, half–naked, but happy. We had faith, we were inspired by high ideals. What kind of ideals do these young people have nowadays, when they never use the word "communist" in their books? Will they be able to prepare the rising generation for the trials that may be in store?

Long Live 1937!

Prior to that Dementiev spoke about the thirties. This veteran accused the television networks of being a prey to sensationalism and "sacrilege" on the occasion of Pushkin's 150th birthday, remarking that: "For the 100th birthday in 1937 the celebration had been more dignified. . . ." . It goes without saying that no mention was made of the purges and "terror" in the 1930s. S. Borzunov, however, went so far as to imply that the ban on the work of recently rehabilitated writers was perhaps justified:

> Some chief editors see it as their main purpose not to raise the level of publications from the ideological and artistic point of view . . . but something else. They have to surprise the reader in finding books that were written in the past but were not published in this country, or were published over there in the West. They do not even trouble to ask why they were not published in their days. In their minds, the fact itself is all that matters. And now a sort of competition has started between them to discover those works and publish them in their journals. The remarkable thing is that it is taking place during the jubilee year of Soviet power!

All this had already been debated during the revelations of 1956 and destalinization. N. Shundik recalled the evil days:

> Many of the actions taken at present remind one of events which occurred immediately after the 20th Party Congress. During one of our literary meetings I spoke then of the confusion between two things: one the wind blowing in the sails of our ship; the other the vessel being tossed about. Some of our "revolutionaries" want us to believe that the roll of the ship is a revolutionary process.

A last look at the *pièce de résistance* by Yuri Bondarev states:

> I would compare the present situation in Russian literature, under siege from the activities of totalitarian and destructive critics, with that of July 1941 when forces, trying to resist in an uncoordinated way, were retreating from the assaults of civilized barbarians. . . . If the retreat goes on and another Stalingrad does not occur, our national values and our pride as a people will disappear into an abyss. Literary pseudo–democrats have lit a torch of *glasnost* on the edge of a chasm, after stealing it from Justice and Truth. This stolen *glasnost* is wrongly portrayed in our media and the press, which show only its destructive and offensive aspect and open wide the doors to mediocrity, by allowing vain talentless newcomers and pseudo–Jacobins to enter.

This extraordinary display of grievances, beyond petty rancours and personal frustrations, allows a glimpse of the line of action adopted by opponents to the new policies. Despite official orders, tongues must remain disciplined in the USSR. There is no question of publicly opposing the directives issued by Gorbachev, so long as they are approved by the whole leadership and officially ratified by various CC plenums. *Perestroika, glasnost,* and even "revolution" are given their due. However, they acquire entirely different meanings. The old guard agrees to the need to revitalize society, as was always the case in Party pronouncements under Stalin, or Khrushchev or Brezhnev. The call for *glasnost* is also fully endorsed, since Lenin was the first to use the word. But it must be done in a spirit of continuity without cancelling anything of the past. The first practical conclusion is that under no circumstances must the "wise old men" (former leaders) be attacked; they are guardians of double talk, and since with varying degrees of success they all served the Party faithfully, they must be respected. This means that their positions and privileges are unassailable and that they deserve them much more than any current supporters of *glasnost.*

Pamiat' and Russian Nationalists

Another kind of opponents used *glasnost* to vent their reckless claims. Even if they are not a mere continuation of Stalinism, they have nothing to do with Gorbachev. They are Russian nationalists who could be called "Slavophiles" as opposed to "Westerners," and who follow the traditional lines of Russian history. In the 1960s and 1970s these chauvinist, racist, and anti–Semitic elements had infiltrated a respectable organization, the association for the protection of historical monuments founded by Academician Likhachev, a man who stood in the forefront of Gorbachev's reforms.

Since then these neo–Slavophiles left for another association, then officially unrecognized, *Pamiat'* (Memory). It was founded in 1980 and attracted public notice in 1987 after 400 members marched through the center of Moscow to ask to be received by Boris Yeltsin, first secretary in Moscow. The request was granted, which was used against him at the start of an inquiry in November 1987. In some respects *Pamiat'* members act in accordance with the new policy since they are against corruption and want the clean–up to go much further. They even want some retired officials "shot," as a *Pamiat'* activist stated in an interview given to a Soviet newspaper.[15]

In other respects, though, they stand poles apart from the new policies. They are anti–Semitic, they advocate emigration of Soviet Jews to Israel, and disagaree with allowing emigrés to come back if they change their minds. This happened in a few cases which were given wide publicity for propaganda reasons. Their anti–Western attitude does not agree with present–day diplomacy and Party slogans either. Significantly the sharpest attacks against *Pamiat'* can be found in *Ogoniok* and *Moscow News*.

This example proves that not all opponents of Gorbachev are intellectuals or *apparatchiki*. Down the social ladder appears another kind. Much hostility was provoked by measures against alcoholism, which for many meant more queues, knowing well there were no shortages. Most bread queues were part of daily life in the USSR, but the average consumer (not necesarily a drunkard) sees more vexation in queues for alcohol, which are artificially imposed from above. Gorbachev is, therefore, blamed even if other leaders are even more fiercely opposed to alcoholism than he.

Another source of resentment is a new system of quality controls in factories where there appeared inspectors of a new administration early in 1987, the Gospriemka, to check on goods ready for delivery. This put an end to many old practices by the hierarchy, but also by ordinary employees, of bonuses. Disorders broke out as a result since bonuses were lost. They may have been provoked by excessive zeal of inspectors who were not always blameless, as Gorbachev suggested in his report to the plenum in January 1987:

> There were some who were defeated by their mission. Instead of tackling the problem through hard work, they frightened themselves and others by brandishing the possibility of all kinds of complications, conflicts with the work force, and even stoppages.[16]

In short, apart from the minority fringes of the intelligentsia and the press, the population has seen so far more inconveniences than advantages in *perestroika*. Undoubtedly a section of the population was pleased to see some of the tyrants bite the dust; and the drive against corruption is also popular, so long as it is not directed against the illegal arrangement a majority of the Soviet people are tied to in order to overcome the difficulties of daily life. Lastly, the experience of many energetic but short–lived campaigns to enforce labor discipline raised a great deal of skepticism in the silent majority, which remains much more impervious to the "Gorbachev effect" than its Western equivalent.

Raisa, An Asset or a Liability?

As the reaction of a large part of Soviet dissidents living in the West shows, the average Soviet citizen attaches little importance to his leaders' personalities. He sees them as anonymous and interchangeable figures. He may have rejoiced over the downfall of the sick old men who brought into disrepute the Party and the state, but he does not respond to the charismatic appeal of the new Secretary General and even less so to his attractive wife, Raisa, who is greatly admired in the West. In Soviet society, which is completely male oriented, a woman's place is either at work, as testified by the huge proportion of women in many professions, or at home. Television appearances of Raisa did not make as good an impression in the USSR as they did in the West. On the contrary, they were seen almost as a shameful boast, which women in particular resented as "exhibitionism" and a proof of frivolity on her part. In an interview given to the Moscow correspondent of the *New York Times*, one of Gorbachev's associates admitted that the position occupied by Raisa Gorbacheva seems "unsuitable" to many people and that the wife of the Secretary General "has become a problem." But he added that "it would be a mistake to turn around at this stage."[17]

Naturally the conservative elements in the apparatus know how to put to capital use these popular feelings and put a spoke in the wheels of Gorbachev's reform movement. The KGB also is willing to exploit the moods of the public.

Chapter IX

POLICE AND ARMES FORCES

With or without *glasnost*, the police retain their role and importance in the USSR. Since the days of Brezhnev there has been little change in their duties and in the various organizations or ministries concerned: Ministry of the Interior or MVD, which covers uniformed police (militia), the territorial army, camp, better known as Gulag guards, firemen, etc. The Committee for State Security, the famous KGB, deals with intelligence at home and counterespionage and spying activities abroad (CIA and FBI in the United States), while it also has its own armed forces and a large body of border militia under its command; finally there is the military police and the department of military intelligence (GRU) involved in policing.

Among these institutions, the MVD is the largest, the KGB the most powerful and, up to now, the most prestigious. Stalin consolidated his dictatorship by means of the KGB (rather the NKVD as it was then known), a pliable instrument in his hands. Its apparatus and incriminating files on the *nomenklatura* stored in its offices enabled Andropov to defeat Cernenko. Thus, all succession problems need KGB's assent, at least tacit, to be solved.

Gorbachev's assumption to power in March 1985 was no exception. After Chernenko's death, and perhaps even a year earlier at the time of the previous succession, the present Secretary General was KGB's choice. It was Andropov's decision, and his associate and heir Cherbikov, chairman of the KGB since 1982, could hardly go back on it.

To start with, there is evidence that Gorbachev only received lukewarm support. Of course, the countless rumors circulating in the USSR cannot all be the result of the KGB's campaigns of disinformation. However, when they concern the head of state and are passed on to foreigners posted in Moscow, their likelihood of being KGB's plants becomes stronger. From the summer of 1986 a new type of rumor came to the knowledge of foreign correspondents. First, they concerned an assassination attempt on Gorbachev while touring the Far East in the Soviet Union. This rumor may have started after Gorbachev voiced more radical ideas of reforms during a meeting with writers in June 1986. Referring to foreign adversaries, the Secretary General said:

> Only one thing worries them: the growth of democracy in our country. . . . This is why they wage a full–scale war against our leadership, which can even mean terrorism. They evoke the apparatus, which broke Khrushchev, and can once again break the new leadership.[1]

These were ambiguous words, combining a reference to foreign in-spired "terror," with an allusion to opposition from the Russian "ap-paratus" and Khrushchev's downfall. Everyone knows that none was caused by "imperialism." This statement was sufficient to fuel rumors of assassination attempts which were admitted in private by other leaders. The same thing happened a year later when the *Bildzeitung*, a German weekly, published information from a KGB source on food poisoning of the Secretary General during his long summer holidays in 1987.

In 1986 unkind gossip was circulating about Raisa Gorbacheva: she lived extravagantly, built a luxurious dacha at public expense, had applied for the position of Minister of Culture, etc. As we know, the sexist climate in the USSR is enough to explain such nonsense. But public opinion could not be responsible for the news of a video-cassette containing the misdemeanors of the Secretary General's wife circulating in Moscow, exhibiting her behavior during trips abroad.[2] No foreigner has ever seen the film in question, but the fact that it was mentioned to correspondents of the "bourgeois" press cannot be without political significance.

There was also the Daniloff affair. An American journalist was arrested and put into jail by the KGB in the summer of 1986. Cu-riously enough, at the time relations with the United States were improving so much so that the Reykjavik summit became possible in October. The affair was similar to past attempts by some police chiefs to face the leader of the day with a *fait accompli*. Khrushchev experienced the same embarrassment when a German diplomat was attacked in a Moscow church in the summer of 1964 while he was trying to improve relations with Bonn. It looked as if the changes that the Secretary General was bringing about in foreign policy were being sabotaged. A little later, on December 8, 1986, one of the most famous dissidents, Anatoli Marchenko, died in his place of internment under suspicious circumstances, just as a wave of liberation of political prisoners was underway. The KGB—at least some of its top leaders—were probably doing their best for the new policies to misfire.

This may explain why the KGB was treated more roughly in the second stage of Gorbachev's reforms late in 1986 and early in 1987. At this time *Pravda* gave full details on an affair in the autumn of 1986 which received scant coverage. It concerned a journalist of the Voroshilovgrad region in the Ukraine who was arrested and detained in July 1986 for revealing scandals in which local personalities were implicated. The Party daily indicated that one of the culprits was one Dichenko, candidate member of the Party regional committees, but it was not until a few days later that his real function was made public. He was head of the KGB at Voroshilovgrad. The news appeared in a communiqué signed by Viktor Chebrikov, chairman of the KGB for the USSR, who announced the arrest of the culprit and advised his chief in Kiev, Stepan Mukha "to start disciplinary proceedings against his associates in the Voroshilovgrad region."[3] (Mukha was sacked in May 1987.) Probably it was the first time since the institution of the Soviet regime that the KGB, a successor of the *Cheka* and the sinister NKVD, was publicly arraigned for its misdeeds. At the same time the militia was thoroughly "restructured" after the disgrace and suicide of Shchelokov, its leader, and one of Brezhnev's close associates. (He was under investigation for ordering torture of suspects in Karelia.) Thus, Party organs themselves had to comply with *perestroika*. The January plenum upheld a resolution in which the KGB was not mentioned by name but which requested:

> . . . improving the mentality of cadres of the security organs, training them in behaving in a way more appropriate to the climate of increasing democracy and *glasnost*. They must remember that those who are in charge of security have to be blameless in matters of the Law, the Party, and the People.[4]

Did the new directives and the revelation of the Voroshilovgrad scandal originate from Andropov's successor, Chebrikov? Nothing is less sure. Changes at the top in the KGB did follow but were smaller than in other sectors in the two years of Gorbachev's power, until then, a first vice president was replaced (out of two), three or four vice presidents (out of ten), and local bosses in five republics.

Mathias Rust's Cessna: An Unfortunate Occurrence

There is a long history of disasters in Soviet air space. The spy syndrome and climate of red alert, encouraged by the authorities at all times, made any air incursion a highly explosive matter with far reaching consequences. In 1960, Gary Powers, an American pilot of the U–2 spy plane was shot down and captured, resulting in a full–scale crisis between Moscow and Washington. The affair consummated the rift between the USSR and China, and nearly caused Khrushchev to fall from power. In 1983, the flight over the Sakhalin Islands by a South Korean plane making a regular flight led to the death of 269 passengers and crew, not to mention the upheavals caused in the higher ranks of military command with the actions taken by the dying Andropov firing its chiefs.

Under these circumstances, and in spite of the more relaxed atmosphere of the Gorbachev era, it was expected that the young German pilot, Mathias Russ, who violated Russian airspace on May 28, 1987, would cause a scandal. He had taken off from Helsinki in a Cessna. He landed on the evening of the same day right in the middle of Red Square for all the tourists to see. Before landing, he flew his Cessna over the Kremlin several times as well as over the Holy of Holies and the Senate building to be visible to the Politburo members assembled there on their regular Thursday schedule. The meeting had been postponed since Mikhail Gorbachev happened to be in East Berlin on that day for a Warsaw Pact meeting. The affair is and remains a source of embarrassment for it was unprecedented and admirably executed. Even the date was perfect, since it was Ascension Day in the West and "Frontier Guards Day" in the East, which called for elaborate celebrations. On the same evening some frontier guards were arrested in a Moscow park while in a state of intoxication, a sign of prevailing laxity. In any event, when Gorbachev came back to Moscow he decided to strike hard. Two days later at a special session of the Politburo it was decided to dismiss "for negligence and lack of organization" the officer in charge of air defense, Air Marshal Koldunov, who had been in the job for nine years. The

Party leadership was more careful about the Minister of Defense, old Marshal Sokolov, merely stating that a new man would be appointed to "strengthen" the team in charge of the ministry. However, it was announced in the same issue of *Pravda* that the minister had been retired by decree.[5] A fortnight later, a third air marshal, Anatoli Konstantinov, who had been in command of the Moscow regional air defense for seven years and who had recently left the job, was publicly reprimanded.

All these sanctions were unprecedented. Nothing similar had occurred since Zhukov's dismissal for "bonapartism" in 1957. For thirty years no general had been criticized, not to mention fired, and even Sokolov's retirement was a novelty. A law passed under Brezhnev made it impossible for any officer above the rank of colonel general to serve as a reserve officer. He, therefore, remained in active service enjoying all privileges until his death. He might even be given such a sinecure, for example, as the job of "Chief Inspector." In May 1987, Admiral Gorshkov and Marshal Tolubko, former commanders of the Navy and Strategic Missiles, aged seventy–seven and seventy–three respectively, were chief inspectors at the Defense ministry and members of the Central Committee. Marshal Moskalenko, who died in June 1985 at the age of eighty–three, was also chief inspector.

Soon another blow was struck at Army hierarchy when Sokolov's successor to the ministry of Defense was not a marshal but only an army general and, in Party ranks, a candidate member of the Central Committee. General Yazov had been posted in Moscow two months earlier following his command of the Far Eastern military region. He became deputy minister in charge of cadres to outrank all the marshals in active sevice, three first deputy ministers and nine deputy ministers. This was a hard blow to those who saw themselves as favorites for Sokolov's succession: the first deputy ministers Akhromeev and Lushev. The former Chief of General Staff who accompanied Gorbachev at the meeting with Reagan at Reykjavik and had made a good impression on the Americans through his ability as a military diplomat was thought to have been devoted to the Head of State. The latter had enjoyed a brilliant career and had been in command of the two most prestigious military regions (Moscow and the Soviet troops in East Germany), before becoming number two or three at the Ministry.

However, the most flagrant insult was administered to the officers of the Moscow air defense when they were interrogated. The ordeal took place early in June, apparently in the absence of the high command, except for General Lizichev, the head of the political department, but in the presence of Boris Yeltsin who was still first Party Secretary in Moscow. Here are excerpts from his address as published in the official press:

> *Perestroika* has left the military region untouched as nothing has since the 27th congress. The region's command clings to the old ways, and they are afraid of new ideas. Appointments are made to serve immobilism, the old boys' network, and individual whims. . . . A disastrous climate can be observed at all levels: superiors shout insults to their subordinates and they humiliate them as human beings. . . . A climate of self–satisfaction and boastfulness has spread everywhere. . . . Here we are at square one as regards *perestroika*. The Party braced itself to admit to the whole world that our society is in a state of crisis, but in the military region they go on saying: All is well, all is well! The event we have just witnessed, however, heralds the beginning of *perestroika* for the region.[6]

Even in the West it is unusual to hurl such harsh criticism at generals. But in the USSR it was unheard of to have the Red Army and its leaders so shamefully exposed. It is true that for some time signs of growing irritation towards the army had become evident in ruling circles since it had failed to start its own *perestroika*. In March 1987, during a meeting of Party activists at the Defense Ministry, it was observed that the armed forces "are just setting on a long and arduous road of reforms." The minutes concluded:

> Much remains to be done on the part of the General Staff and the political command. Prolonged stagnation was caused by the fact that a whole generation of cadres was educated in an atmosphere of diminished vigilance. Speakers in turn complained that too much consideration was given to administrative methods and not enough attention was paid to the internal reasons of the negative influences that plague us.[1]

The minutes did not strike a new chord in their phrasing, but merely used the official language of *perestroika*, the novelty was that it applied to the military. The army was no longer immune from *perestroika*, and it is not surprising under the circumstances that Gorbachev exploited the Cessna incident to encourage the process and alter the modus vivendi which existed between the new leadership and the marshals after Chernenko's death.

The End of Modus Vivendi

As far as the Secretary General was concerned, his major handicap was an almost total lack of military experience and contact with the armed forces. Unlike all his predecessors, he had not fought in the war, nor had he done his national service. Neither was he involved in defense industry. His only dealing with the army had been purely formal and had come later as first Party Secretary of the Stavropol territory, he was entitled to take part in meetings of the Military Council of the North Caucasian military region. It should be said in passing that he made useful contacts among the officers there, and did not forget them subsequently. The commander of the region at the time, General Belikov, was appointed to the highest position in the Red Army—the command of Soviet forces in East Germany in 1986. Unfortunately for the Secretary General he died suddenly in November 1987.

But the military side lacked charismatic leaders. After Ustinov's death and Marshal Ogarkov's ousting, none of the professional offices were strong personalities or enjoyed much prestige. The officer corps was regarded among Brezhnev's successors as having had their way far too long. The country's resources had been strained and sometimes squandered in ill-advised military ventures. Sometimes the military proved unnecessarily provocative to the West, such as the deployment of SS-20. It should also be added that the affair of the South Korean Boeing did little to enhance army prestige. They were blamed not so much for the death of passengers as they were for their delayed intervention and inability to unravel the ins and outs of what was described as "imperialist provocation."

Thus, when Ustinov died in December 1984, the army leaders ceased to occupy the same position as before in the hierarchy of the Party and the State. This was already apparent in March 1985 at Chernenko's funeral when the Marshals were not among the officials standing on the podium. The trend was confirmed with the appointment of Sokolov as defense minister. He became a candidate member of the Politburo, not a full member as his other predecessors since Grechko in 1973.

The next step was for Gorbachev to assert his authority as Secretary General and chairman of the Defense Council. This obscure organ, which serves as "Army Politburo," makes all the decisions on security, the organization of armed forces, armament programs, and possibly disarmament. This was achieved on July 10, 1985 at Minsk during a "meeting with army commanding officers.[8] In contradiciton with the new rulings of *glasnost*, Gorbachev's address did not appear in the press at the time and has not been published since; neither were the names of the participants disclosed. This may be due to the presence of Marshal Ogarkov who was dismissed a few months earlier from his appointment of Chief-of-Staff and whose new position as commanding officer of the Western military theater has never been officially announced.

One can only guess at the conditions of the *modus vivendi* which was established at the time between the new Party leadership and the army, which remained effective until the Cessna incident two years later. Only some elements of this accommodation are found for, politically, the army had to accept a less prominent position and make sacrifices in the negotiations on disarmament. Talks with the United States were resumed in March 1985 in Geneva, and a few weeks later, on his visit to Paris, Gorachev made the first concessions on Euromissiles. It can be assumed that the Secretary General was already doing his best to persuade the marshals to give up the SS-20 which was developed during the 1970s and was responsible for the Western response after 1983 on Pershing and Cruise missiles for NATO. It may be that the firm stand taken by the Western powers, which seems to have come as a surprise to Brezhnev's strategists, had greatly assisted Gorbachev in his dealings with the high command. However, it was not all clear sailing.

This was revealed in the period after the Reykjavik summit when Soviet policy proposed once again its rigid "package" deals. They made the agreement on Euromissiles dependent on the United States giving up their strategic defense project of Star Wars which was favored by President Reagan. Everything remained at a standstill for several months to the great satisfaction of marshals and probably of Gromyko, who was losing the ground his diplomacy had defended for years.

However, the pause was of short duration. On February 28, 1987, Gorbachev succeeded in untying the "package," making an agreement possible. The Secretary General may have wrenched concessions from

the military in exchange for ending the moratorium he had unilater-
ally imposed on Soviet nuclear tests in August 1985, just after the
Minsk meeting. On February 26, two days before the agreement on
Euromissiles was accepted, Soviet technicians went ahead with nuclear testing for the first time in nineteen months.

Politically, the military were not involved in *perestroika*. They
may have spoken of it like everyone else and pretended to change their
ways. However, at the January 1987 plenum, Gorbachev made just
one point in his report about Soviet armed forces who "also apply the
policy of *perestroika*." It was missing in the final resolution.

In the rank and file the only practical effect of the new policy
seems to have been greater attention paid to the so-called "attesta-
tion." According to it officers have their careers and performances
periodically reviewed by their superiors. Yet the high command remained outside the reorganization which took place in other corps.
Thus, until the purge following the Cessna incident, the three top
jobs in the Defense Ministry were still in the hands of the people chosen by Chernenko: Sokolov (Minister), Akhromeev (Commander-of-
Services) and Kulikov (Warsaw Pact Commander). The only change
at that level was the addition of Army General Lushev as first Vice
Minister of Defense in replacement of Army General Petrov. Marshal
Ogarkov, ex-Chief-of-Services, was kept strictly away from Moscow
 for what was probably considered "rebellion'" against the Politburo
in 1984. Gorbachev and his associates may have been willing to adopt
some of Ogarkov's ideas but they were weary of the man who was seen
as overly ambitious, difficult to work with, and egocentric.

Lower down the rank, until the May–June purge in 1987, the
situation was slightly different. Four vice ministers out of eleven were
replaced, two of them falling as early as 1985, including Marshal Tolubko, who was in charge of strategic missiles and who joined the
Inspector Corps in July 1985 at the time of the Minsk meeting. It
may be that the dismissal was a snub to the policy of "all out nuclear"
forces, which had been the policy until then. A little later Admiral
Gorshkov, navy chief for thirty years, was sent off without any explanation. Still in 1985, Army General Yepishev, who had been head
of the political department of the armed forces for the past twenty-
three years, left his post. He was a typical representative both of the
gneration of "neo-Stalinist cadres" (he worked in the security organs
in the early fifties) and of years of stagnation.

Still lower down, changes took place in the command of the four fleets of the Soviet Navy, of the Red Army groups in GDR, Poland and Hungary, and in eleven military regions. However, military leaders changed jobs more often than civilians, even under Brezhnev, and cadre movements do not seem much more important at the time than in earlier periods. Moreover, apart from Yepishev, who died a few weeks after his dismissal, most of the purged dignitaries kept Party offices, such as ex-vice ministers Tolubko and Gorshko.

Meanwhile, Gorbachev was appointing new members to the Defense Council. This institution is an offshoot of the Politburo and meets to discuss matters of security and armament. General officers are in the minority. Opposite the Defense Minister and the Chief-of-Staff (whose presence may not be automatic), the Council includes the Party Secretary in charge of heavy industry and armaments, the Government deputy-chairman, who presides over the military-industrial commission, as well as some other ministers who deal with armament programs, bearing certain esoteric and coded names that are impossible to pronouce. As an example, the minister for "General Machine Guilding" (*Minobschmach*) looks after the manufacture of all strategic missiles; another "Medium Machine Building" (*Minredmach*) produces nuclear warheads for the missiles.

All the ministries servicing the Military-Industrial complex changed hands in the first two years of the new leaders. The secretary in charge of the Defense Industry was Grigory Romanov, Gorbachev's rival, who fell early in July 1985. He was replaced by Lev Zaikov, aged sixty-two, who had previously succeeded Romanov as head of the Leningrad Party. He was then promoted to the Politburo and remained the third "super secretary" for a long time. He was later transferred to Moscow City to replace Yeltsin.

In the government structure, the Military-Industrial Commission was taken from Leonid Smirnov's hands in November 1985. The latter was a veteran of the armament industry, appointed in Stalin's days. Yuri Masliukov, who had been first vice chairman of Gosplan, took over. The top man for the missile industry, Oleg Baklanov, kept his job, although he had been appointed under Andropov in April 1983. This was different for his fellow minister for nuclear warheads, Yefim Slavsky, who headed *Minredmach* since 1957. He hung on until November 1986 when he gave way reluctantly to his deputy, Lev Ryabev. Like most of Brezhnev's ministers, Smirnov was nearly seventy when he left in 1985; his successor, Masliukov, was forty-eight then and is still the youngest deputy chairman. Ryabov, who was born in 1933, could have been his predecessor's grandson. Slavsky was eighty-eight years old in 1986, which made him the oldest minister in the USSR and probably in the world. If the high command was roughly unchanged since Chernenko, downstream the effects of *perestroika* were more visible, especially in the Military-Industrial complex. It was evident that the Ministry of Medium Machine Building came under fire after the Chernobyl disaster and was completely reorganized, more so than any other administration dealing with nuclear industry. Alexander Meshkov, first vice minister, was dismissed in July for "serious errors and shortcomings" before being "severely reprimanded at the Party level."[9] Undoubtedly other specialists in civil nuclear power industry went down with him, but he was the highest in rank as well as candidate member of the Central Committee. However, the army succeeded in "eliminating the consequences of the Chernobyl accident" for which it was blamed. It is possible that "experiments" recklessly carried out by the personnel of the power station had been ordered and controlled by the *Minsredmach* authorities for defense purposes.

The Law of Maximum Allocation

The most likely component of the *modus vivendi* between Gorbachev and the army was to its advantage since it continued to receive roughly the same amount of resources. It is impossible to gauge it with any accuracy, but let us join in the game played by world experts who try to estimate the proportion of military expenditure in the budget of the Soviet Union. Naturally in terms of actual expenditure, not the grossly undervalued official budget which has recently been shown to cover only salaries and pensions, not the purchase of equipment or research: 11 percent, 13 percent, or 25 percent? Estimates fluctuate, say some specialists, such as those of the CIA, who are revising theirs drastically all the time.

It seems simpler to start from the principle that, from the beginning of the Brezhnev era at least and in all likelihood in the aftermath of the Cuban missile crisis in 1962, the USSR decided to give the army the greatest share of available resources. It follows that the total amount of allocations for national security would not be cut, but its share of global figures would not increase. A ceiling had to be set because the growth of the economy had slowed down. Up to the mid-seventies, it was quite satisfactory and huge armament programs could be launched as well as all sorts of strategic systems developed.

Everything went fine until "the West woke up" after the Afghanistan invasion and the discovery of the SS–20s. Increases in military spending for the NATO forces were rushed through in response. The trend was accentuated when President Reagan arrived at the White House in 1981. This period coincided with a slowdown in the Soviet economy, followed by stagnation. New technologies ("sophisticated" classical weapons) and their development by the Pentagon (Star Wars), forced the Soviet military to turn to the Politburo for new funds to meet these challenges.

Certain Politburo conservatives wished to strengthen the nuclear component. Others, led by Ogarkov, wanted to slow down nuclear programs, but they requested a fresh injection of resources to extend, diversify, and modernize conventional weapons. Since the law of "maximum effort" made any flexibility impossible, Brezhnev himself in his last speech to the high command in October 1982, had to make it clear that the amount of global resources could not be raised. They should put existing resources to better use. It may be that Marshal Ogarkov's repeated his demands in the following year and for that reason was dismissed by Chernenko in 1984.

Up to that time the same law of maximum effort did, of course, apply to Gorbachev. The tough measures taken against the top ranks of the military hierarchy probably helped the Secretary General to make his views on expenditures prevail. His appropriation was the same, but the funds were distributed in a different manner—less on "heavy nuclear" and more on "advanced conventional" weapons, putting the emphasis on quality rather than quantity. Significantly, the new technologies of lasers and computing sciences were given a fresh impetus after 1985.

Nonetheless, Gorbachev gave the high command a better sense of direction both in financial matters and their relations to political power. In the preceding years, the lethargy which gripped the Party leadership could have made the high command take a closer look at the government of the country, and since it was bankrupt come up its own ideas for remedies. The temptation, that is if it ever existed, has now vanished, since Gorbachev, an *apparatchik*, in his overall reform is trying to reform the Party as well. Yet several years of another Chernenko might well awaken it.

Chapter X

THE SUMMIT: PERSONAL POWER
OR COLLECTIVE LEADERSHIP?

It is easy to believe Mikhail Gorbachev when he describes the difficulties encountered by his reforming policies. However, we often rather naively believe him when he asserts that his authority is not threatened by an internal opposition. All Party leaders unanimously support the new political line, he confidently stated in September 1987 upon his return from holiday that "there is no political opposiiton."

True enough there are no parties competing with the Communist Party and no easily identified groupings or tendencies within it. The last remnant of what we in the West would call pluralism was eliminated by Lenin in the 1920s under the shameful label of "fractionism." Yet it would be a mistake to assume that the political leadership or the population are as "monolithic" as they are supposed to be.

Even under Stalin, fierce encounters occurred between his closest associates under an impulse common to all mankind that was overlooked by Marx: the struggle for power. Zhdanov and Malenkov clashed fiercely. The latter was in turn defeated by Khrushchev in the 1950s. Later still Kirilenko and Chernenko clashed, and again the latter and Andropov were opposed. The power struggle is ongoing at all periods, and particularly in times of reform. The so-called "conservatives" are simply content with slowing down the implementation of new policies, and they try to influence decision making at the very top, which is not and cannot be unanimous or monolithic. To demonstrate this argument, two institutions are examined—the Central Committee and its Politburo.

The Party "Parliament"

If the Central Committee was often referred to as the Parliament of the Party, it should not be mistaken for its democratic equivalents in the West. This parliament is under close surveillance and does not meet mandatorily more than twice a year for incredibly short periods—two or three days under Khrushchev—and it took two weeks of an extraordinary session in 1957 for the Central Committee to reverse the Politburo's decisions and keep Khrushchev in power. Yet it took less than half a day for the same man, Khrushchev, to be dismissed in 1964. Since then, the Party parliament was kept by Brezhnev within narrow confines, and for over twenty years no plenum exceeded a day. "Democratization," as decreed by Gorbachev, has made an impact for since that time several plenums held since 1987 lasted two days. It should be added that the debates are not published, unlike those of Khrushchev's days.

This being so, the Central Committee, with some 300 full members and 150 candidates, is the focal point of the *nomenklatura*, the place where the heart of the apparatus beats. Not everyone is able to speak from the rostrum, but the corridors of power are alive with rumors and resentments which the supreme leadership has to take into account. This is a body where the reform movement led by Gorbachev has no great majority. In 1986, 172 out of 307 re–elected members are survivors of the last congress under Brezhnev in 1981, and 116, or almost a third, had the same job ten years earlier.

It is true that most members of the present Politburo, and Gorbachev himself, are in this group. The "hard core" of opposition to Gorbachev is also found among these veterans who are the guardians of the temple and complain most vehemently about unheavals caused by *perestroika* and *glasnost*.

Since April 1985, over 30 Central Committee members retired or were dismissed from their official posts. This means that they cannot implement the new policies but can still sit in the Party Parliament and express their views. To this list must be added a small group of dignitaries who have lost their positions since 1985 but were given minor jobs, such as "State Councillor with the Council of Ministers" (Baibakov, ex–chairman of the Planning Commission), or with the presidium of the Supreme Soviet, (Tikhanov, premier under Brezhnev) where he keeps company with Grishin under the protective wing of Gromyko). Finally, there are some top military men: Admiral

Gorshkov, Commander of the Navy for thirty years, and Marshal To-bulko, in charge of strategic missiles, both of whom were appointed inspectors.

All in all, many members out of power still retained their seats on the Central Committee, constituting more than one–tenth of the total Brezhnev era which they represented. What can a man like Baibakov, for example, think and say on the economic reorganization that is taking place when he is the archetype of the kind of planning practiced under Stalin and Brezhnev? What attitudes can Tikhonov or Ponomarev, two relics of the old era, adopt in the Central Com-mittee? It is difficult to imagine that they do not make use of their right to speak, or of the many friends they still have in the corridors of power, to criticize or even thwart the Secretary General's reforms.

For this reason Gorbachev cannot be satisfied with a Central Committee which does not have enough new blood to support him. Before the statutory five years are over he has to hold another congress to effect the necessary changes, and he has to improvise. In his day, Khrushchev tried to consolidate his 1957 victory by convening an "extraordinary" congress in 1959. He wanted the assembly to elect a new Central Committee without waiting for the 1961 deadline. But he did not succeed, and if the congress gathered, it held no elections. One man opposed the move, Suslov. He insured the re–election to have no fear of all those elected in 1956 and not expelled in 1957. The ebullient new Party chief, Khrushchev, was checked.

The curious thing is that Suslov himself had entered the Central Committee through extraordinary measures. He was one of the few promoted by the National Conference held in 1941, a few months before the USSR entered the war. This is an interesting precedent for there has not been another Party conference since that time.

EPILOGUE

What Kind of Power, and to What End?

It is now three years since the book was first written, four years since the start of *perestroika*, and almost six years since Gorbachev assumed power. After these eventful years—far more momentous than could be expected back in 1987—what is the situation in the USSR?

First, we are faced with a paradox. Mid-way through 1989 the Soviet Union was pioneering *perestroika* within the "socialist system." It had forged ahead of its satellites and was taking huge strides in implementing reforms, while the "dinosaurs" of the Stalin–Brezhnev era—such as Honeker, Zhivkov, Ceausescu, and the like—were dragging their feet. Today the torch of progress is in the possession of other counries; the USSR has been overtaken by its disciples.

A striking feature of the different evolution of the old satellites and the Soviet Union is the speed with which reforms are carried out in the former, while the country where *perestroika* was first introduced is taking a long time in reforming its system. Such *appartchiks* as Egon Krenz in East Germany, Urbanek in Czechoslovakia, and Grosz in Hungary were obviously unable to cling to power because of past misdeeds. They had to withdraw after a few weeks, but, seen from a Soviet point of view, these leaders of the "new look socialist revolution" showed a high degree of realism. They were fully aware of the need to discard, together with their national "dinosaurs," most of the Stalinist legacy—the party monopoly of power, Lenin's myth of "democratic centralism." In many cases Marxism itself, has been thrown to the wind in the space of a few days, at worst a few weeks. This course was also followed by the few *apparatchiks* still in power today.

Nothing of the sort occurred in the Soviet Union. A multi–party system is emerging gradually, but alongside a remarkably rigid set of

Stalinist institutions. In February 1990, the international press hailed as a great achievement the fact that the validity of Article 6 of the Soviet constitution guaranteeing "the leading role of the communist party" was tested in the Supreme Soviet and found wanting. Yet few people bothered to notice that several years of *glasnost* had been necessary to bring about the examination of the article. In any case the article was fairly recent and was written into the constitution by Brezhnev in 1976. Neither Lenin nor Stalin felt any need for it when they instituted a totalitarian system. So presumably many such "victories" will be needed before the promised "rule of law" is the norm.

In every other respect the USSR remains behind the old satellite countries, and the implementations of the main components of the economic reform have been either postponed or are still being debated and amended out of recognition. The draft legislation on land ownership avoids the fateful "private property" phrase and its first draft, acclaimed in February 1990 as "re-establishing peasant ownership," only considers the handing over of leases—inheritance included—not full ownership by the peasants. The principle of a market economy had made some progress, but only in words. There is no question of making the ruble convertible nor of freeing prices in the forseeable future, which in the prevailing circumstances could mean never.

Of course, several basic laws of the "rule of law" finally have been passed. A law on the press makes it possible for a newspaper or even a television broadcasting station to be started by people other than Party members or associated organizations. However, the question of technical equipment, offices, and running costs is left unanswered. In the meantime, what is left of the Party–State keeps its own property. Immediately after its election the progressive Moscow City Council lost 37 buildings through a decree hastily voted by the old authorities. Similarly Gorbachev's decree, which "liberalized" television, made sure that Gosterleradio, the old state organization, did not lose any of its regional stations.

It is clear that things which are unthinkable today will become a reality tomorrow, just as political pluralism developed in society well before it was officially recognized. Yet any progress in democratization or economic reform suffers from the syndrome of "too little and too late," that is, too late especially to bring about solutions of those problems which have all been getting worse.

What are the causes for such long delays? Obviously there are political hurdles to overcome. However, the main body of resistance to reforms in depth is situated in an area other than the "old guard" in the apparatus, which is often blamed for it. First and foremost, society as a whole is involved in the country's reluctance to change. In reality neither the undoubted popular appeal of radical reformers nor the numbers of demonstrators for the reforms should be taken at face value. The man in the street wants nothing better than to send all the old leaders packing, whether at the top or the bottom of the regime, at the center of the Soviet Union or in the regions. After decades of oppression, he has lost faith in Marxism, thinks little of Lenin and slips easily back into his old creed, nationalistic, religious, and cultural. This by no means implies that he is willing to accept the consequences of all the genuine political and economic reforms. As the post–war experience showed in the West and now in Eastern Europe, all reforms lead to the western model of parliamentary democracy and market economy. In the USSR, two factors stand in the way—unlike in Eastern European countries. One is the legacy of seventy years of communism, in turn war communism, then the Stalinist regime, ending with "stagnation," a legacy of levelling of society and a loss of a sense of responsibility. Forty years of communism in the satellite countries were not sufficient to root out old reflexes. Their populations still remember the preceding 'capitalist' era. This national epoch has often been pictured by the old generation in glowing terms as a reaction to the somber recent past or present. In economic development, even a Chinese peasant knows more about private enterprise than the most educated Moscow official, which explains why economic reforms were more successful in China than during the first ten years of the revolutionary regime.

In the USSR, except in the Baltic countries which have also come under communism more recently, all of the past experiences are forgotten. The situation is all the more disastrous because the starting point of development was much lower than in the West, which represents another obstacle to change.

Russia had her entrepreneurial class—a very dynamic one—early in the century, but only for a decade or two. Russian economy really took off around 1910 only to be brutally cut short by the war in 1914 and the revolution in 1917. Even in this short period of expansion, capitalism was only one element in a diversified society whose main components were an enormous peasantry and a small ruling, although declining, aristocracy. The ruling class was itself

divided between idle and obscurantist landlords and more enlight-
ened town dwellers, both of whom unanimously despised the emerging new class of "merchants" (*kupsy*), as they were then still called,
instead of "industrialists" (*promyshlenniki*). The old populist ideal
of egalitarianiasm—always strong among the intelligentsia—obscured
the picture of Russian society still further. Money making, individual
wealth, and private enterprise never held much appeal to the Russians. This constitutes the main difference between them and most of
the East European nations. Undoubtedly, since Peter the Great there
has always been a movement opposed to the Slavophiles, "Westernizers." Their very name shows that they stood for the opposite of the
Slovophiles who favored Russian traditions and untainted Russianness
itself. In fact, both movements suffered from an inferiority complex
towards the West and its riches, but each drew different conclusions.
The Westernizers wanted to imitate their Western model blindly, if
need be even force it on Russia. The Slavophiles believed in a special
mission for Russia devising a specific model which was neither fully
fledged capitalism nor Western parliamentary democracy.

The Western type of democracy, acclaimed as an ideal by East
European countries, is seen in a different light in Russia. It has an
entirely negative value providing an empty framework in which individuals can develop freely, but falls short of providing values which
would satisfy the generous aspirations of the Slavophiles. The basic
principle of the rule of law, that is "Everything is allowed which is
not forbidden by law," hurts the susceptibilities, including not only
the totaliarian diehards who claimed the opposite for decades but
also the Russian moralists who cannot accept that the state be neutral. Solzhenitsyn, for example, who is one of the chief spokesmen
of this trend of thought, holds that morality is more important than
law. Truth in its almost mystical sense (*Istina*, more than the down
to earth *Pravda*), is what the country lacks, not so much freedom.
It seems to him that the Stalinist regime's worst characteristic was
institutionalized lies, a violent repression of society, rather than any
absence of democracy or political pluralism.

At present the Slavophile trend is gaining ground since it seems to
be the only way to salvage something of the Stalin–Brezhnev heritage
(patriotism tainted with chauvinism and xenophobia, and cultural
values unsullied by profit motives), adding to it more respectable
values stemming from the old Marxist thought (religion, economy).
In short, these thinkers are able to re–establish links with the era

prior to communism, without forcing a complete and heartrending break with the more recent past.

The proof of this assertion is in the fact that old "Stalinists" and new "patriots" club together, as well as old bolshevik atheists, closing ranks with new religiously minded conservatives. Many of the former are quite willing to throw overboard their old Marxist–Leninist creed which is clearly bankrupt, to join the latter in upholding old reactionary values. Although presented as instruments of the class struggle, these were always present in communist ideology, that is to say, respect of law and order, hatred of "democrats" and all radicals—not to mention Jews, freemasons or foreigners of all kinds. The excesses of *Pamiat'*, an ultra–nationalist association, only reveal the tip of the iceberg.

This organization is certainly-the backbone of the most determined opposition to *perestroika*. An egalitarian outlook is the source of the well–publicized hostility that cooperatives, early forms of private enterprise, are meeting with. The average Russian prefers denunciation or intrigue to bring back to his level a man who has grown richer rather than imitate him and raise his own standards of living. Another reason is that morality is widely seen as more important than law. No amount of coercion from the authorities nor legislative measures have any impact on this popular belief.

In any event one of the draft laws passed on cooperatives put several limitations on them, one of which was abstaining from "speculation," besides the fact that the term is rather imprecise. The legislators overlooked the effect these restrictions had on the newly created cooperatives, giving them a marginal character and leaving them open to public criticism. As long as they represent only 1 or 2 percent of the economic activity of the country, as is the case now, they will remain exceptions in a sea of shortages and derive unfair advantage from the situation. On the other hand, if their share of the market grows to 10 or 50 percent, they will have a stimulating influence on it and will compete with the nationalized sector. However, is it just that the authorities hold against them, since they play on popular feelings and allow for "ideal" cooperatives only, which are unworkable in practice? It is a vicious circle and it will remain unbroken until the legislators, even those in favor of reforms, find the courage to ignore their own propaganda issues and morality when they are drafting new laws.

Another impediment to changes, such as those seen in Eastern

Europe, is the problem of nationalities. As the last colonial empire on earth, the Soviet Union cannot be democratized, even partially, without having to face identical demands from the many nations which it comprises, resulting in a call for real independence from the peoples subjugated in the past. No Eastern European country, not even Romania with its Hungarian minority, finds itself in the same position. It is one of Mikhail Gorbachev's most blatant miscalculations that he failed to foresee this unavoidable consequence of *glasnost*.

The problem was made more acute, if not created, by political reforms as well as the economic crisis. Before devising the best way to share the national income there has to be wealth to share. In the event of shortages, resentments are such that a person belonging to another minority, either living near by or deported on Stalin's orders, is blamed for difficulties. He is a "parasite" or "black marketeer"—in short a scapegoat who attracts, sometimes with the blessing of the authorities, violent antagonism.

To all this must be added the impact of events in Eastern Europe. On the one hand, many people are saddened by the loss of empire. They are the old generation reared in the days of the "Great Patriotic War" and hatred of Germany. Army personnel used to view East and Central Europe as a buffer zone and exercise grounds, and they all refuse to accept the humiliation the upheaval brought to them. On the other hand, how could the Baltic populations fail to react to the collapse of neighboring communist states, and how could Moldavians—in reality Romanians belonging to the Soviet Union—remain unaffected by the disappearance of Ceausescu who had served as a convenient scapegoat so far? Especially since they had fallen, in both cases, victims to the shameful agreements—disavowed nowdays— entered into by Stalin and Hitler, just like the other "fraternal countries" of liberated Eastern Europe.

Thus, the danger from nationalism facing the central leader, Gorbachev, has many facets. In the Southern Republics (Caucasus and Central Asia) nationalism erupted violently, causing bloodshed in Armenia and Dushanbe through Karabkh and Baku. However, from a political point of view, the solution is easy because the Russian central power and its army are the only forces capable of restoring law and order and ending pogroms, thereby acquiring legitimacy. Even foreign powers prefer law and order, be it of the Soviet variety, to violent disorders and massacres.

It is quite another matter with the Baltic challenge to Soviet power. It is a non–violent movement, heralding the unavoidable break–up of the empire as a whole. The only way left to Gorbachev to avoid the immediate secession of Lithuania and of the other Baltic republics is to send troops in, and this time with no pretense of restoring public order and at the cost of halting political and economic reforms at home and abroad for a long time. The "Brezhnev doctrine" of limited sovereignty was abolished as far as the "external" empire is concerned, but it could not be re–established on the border of the "internal empire," namely in the Baltic countries. It causes considerable damage to the political image of the Soviet leader and the atmosphere of détente in Europe, especially to the "common European home" which has become slightly more credible in recent months.

One has to remember the new sense of national identity enjoyed by the major republics, starting with Russia, which after electing Boris Yeltsin as President and setting up an independent communist party under Polozkov, a conservative, has become an alternative center of power. By the same token, the Ukraine and Byelorussia, followed by most of the Union's republics, proclaimed themselves sovereign or even "neutral." These are, of course, more verbal assertions, but they make the "Federal Pact" dear to Gorbachev seem lesser and lesser. For the time being the latter can only bide his time in dealing with this problem as well as many others, but he is losing ground. Things have reached a point when nobody can hope to have his orders obeyed, and "graduated plans" have lost all credibility. Therefore, it is impossible to envisage, for example, the application of a law on secession, as it provides for a five–year interval between the holding of a referendum in a given republic and ratification of its result by the Congress of Deputies in Moscow. Neither would payment of "financial reparations" to the federation be enforceable on the republics about to leave since it would also apply to those which were annexed in the most brutal manner by Stalin.

Only in the event of a complete turnaround by the Moscow authorities could imminent territorial losses be avoided for the empire. In the long term, however, there may be a ray of hope with the creation of an updated federation, of a voluntary nature, centered around the Slavic republics of Russia, the Ukraine, and Byelorussia. But to entice at least a few of the non–Slavic republics, such a federation should enjoy even looser ties than the United States of America, which have in common cultural affinities and a successful economic system that is totally lacking in the USSR. It seems probable also that nothing of the kind can be set up before the collapse of the old regime, since it is obviously too inflexible to be changed. Most nationalists hold that they have to secede before any step can be taken to reactivate an associative union.

It is important to stress that the problems to be solved in Soviet society act as background to purely political questions. Nowadays Soviet life does not resolve around the all powerful Party and its Holy of Holies, the Politburo, whose only function was to crush society and any manifestations of real life. The latter had come to the fore even under the rule of "stagnation," as facts speak for themselves sooner or later. It is now society's turn to take the limelight, whatever may be the wishes of individuals. Despite the facts, politics is still at the center of the debate since it has retained many of the past characteristics. The chief of these is being dominated by a supposedly charismatic leader who holds more and more of the key functions while being less and less able to control the situation. This contradiction is at the core of all the difficulties facing the USSR in the autumn of 1990.

In reality, Gorbachev, the *apparatchik*, has changed less rapidly than the country at large, so that his repeated warnings to his opponents, who are accused of "fighting for personal power," are in fact directed at himself The man who had first refused the job as Head of State held by his predecessors (in the past a purely honorary one) finally accepted it. Moreover, he had himself elected to the job three times in three years, and each time with increased powers. Besides, at least once a year since 1987, a crisis more serious than the preceding one gave grounds for wondering whether the Secretary General's position was not under threat, whether the "die hards" of the apparatus were not about to seize control again. Each time Mikhail Gorbachev "bounced back" taking a grip of the situation and adding to his already vast power.

Already late in 1988 a crisis ended with the Party Secretariat being divided into "commissions." Ligachev, his main opponent, was partially shelved. Early in 1990 the setting up of a presidential regime curbed the government's power together with that of its head, Nikolai Ryzhkov, who is a potential rival. Then came a serious alert in the following spring when a group of conservatives rebelled and Russian communists rose against their leader, only to be followed by the 28th congress of the federal party deciding—much to eveyone's

surprise—to drop Egor Ligachev and to clean up the Central Committee, weakening the Politburo for good. If the Party came out of
the crisis with ruffled feathers, none of this affected its head, who not
only was confirmed in his position but was the only person to hold
a dual mandate, thereby gaining as the head of state what he lost
as Party leader. How did he achieve this? In the traditional way,
that is securing the trump cards rather than changing the rules of
the game. Initially, like his several predecessors, he tried to modernize the system without tampering with its structures, to motivate
the Party while increasing his influence and prerogatives. But like
them, he had to manoever and strengthen his personal power over
the apparatus and the central leadership he had inherited so that he
isolated and later eliminated his opponents within the Politburo without breaching the statutory regulations of "democratic centralism,"
of collegiate leadership, and cooperation. We know from past experience that this is a task all the more difficult since the leader is more
ambitious—Khrushchev finally floundered while Brezhnev succeeded
after at least six or seven years, and mainly because his only ambition
was to usher in the heyday of *nomenklatura.* The only people who
managed to make the Party serve their own ambition were Stalin,
and later Mao Tse-tung in China—only for a period of time though
in the latter case. To achieve their ends, both had to break up not
only the apparatus but the Party itself and then build a new one over
the ashes of the old.

   It would be a cynical view of *perestroika* to give to Gorbachev
the same motives as those of Stalin or Mao. The main difference is
that, while the two dictators chose to destroy the Party in the name
of revolutionary purity and totalitarian extremism, he does it in the
name of democratization. Another difference is that, while this task
encountered the same obstacles and met with the same reflexes of
"fighting for survival" in a doomed apparatus it has also put in mo-
tion a social process which got out of control and forced on Gorbachev
all manners of choices and decisions at an ever increasing rate that
he could not easily deal with since he was still tied to collegiate leadership. At the top, at least, the methods he used were essentially of
the classical kind. Following in his predecessors' footsteps, Gorbachev
was able to use the enormous prerogatives of his position as Secretary
General, that is a monopoly of taking initiatives, free access to the
media, ability to hold the levers of command of all the organizations
under his control whether legally or otherwise, and the "legitimist"

reflex of most of the conservatives. When all is said and done, the system defended by the "old guard" of the Central Committee is that of democratic centralism, which deprives them of any say in the face of the Secretary General and "collegiate" leadership of the Politburo. As long as this body has not proposed to the "Parliament of the Party" the name of another leader and a new political program, the Central Committee must be content with ratifying whatever comes to it from above for approval. This is, for instance, what it did at the end of its plenum in February 1990 when it voted a "political platform" almost unanimously which had been under criticism by a majority of the speakers. This is the course followed by the Congress in July of the same year when it voted for Gorbachev as head of the Party, although he was politely detested by a majority of the delegates, only because the old Politburo had no other credible candidate to replace him.

Another method has been proven to be worthwhile using, that is when the political situation makes it impossible to purge in the right way the institutions, the latter can be effectively weakened—both in status and competence. As it has been seen, the Party Secretariat often embarrassed Gorbachev, while Ligachev ruled supreme during 1987 and 1988. Hard luck for it, since it was practically abolished late in 1988. Also for the Politburo, a body where—by all accounts—it is even more difficult to oust a member than to have a new one admitted. From early 1990 the unfortunate Politburo lost many of its prerogatives and met infrequently, only to be completely overhauled by the Party Congress a few months later. Of course, all this rests on a basic notion which is respectable, that is shifting power from the Party to the State, as a preliminary to rationalizing institutions. However, this is not the only aim or explanation since the government in this case should have been given pride of place while it has gradually lost its prerogatives to the president, for it could not be radically purged in its membership.

Overall, Gorbachev has managed to shed his opponents faster than any of his predecessors, including Stalin, although he is not given a free hand to do so. An example of this stepping back was demonstrated at the June 1989 Party Conference. It was the first time that an open debate was taking place in the USSR—well before the meeting of the Congress of deputies the following spring, which was to be the first parliamentary debate. The Conference roused wide interest in the country, and public opinion was captivated by it. Inasmuch as it ended in a draw, the resolutions that were passed were no more than "orientations" for the next Party Congress, the statutes were not amended, and the Central Committee was not renewed. It is tempting to draw a parallel with the conference of the fraternal Hungarian party (still the socialist workers' party, therefore communist) held in May 1989, at the same time. These proceedings turned into a congress where Janos Kadar was ousted forever and all members of the Central Committee were replaced, resulting in far reaching reforms and giving Hungary a leading position among East European countries for a growing democracy. In hindsight, Moscow had to admit that a golden opportunity was missed.

In effect the radical changes occurred only two years later at the 28th congress, which means—unfortunately—two years too late. It took five years to liquidate Ligachev, even longer to do the same with Ryzhkov, which is acceptable in comparison with past achievements, but far too long in a context of revolutionary unrest spreading dangerously all over the country. Thus, the time taken by Gorbachev in his struggle for power cannot be used in dealing with more urgent tasks. Hence these years, which would normally represent a formidable feat of political skill, amount to a long list of missed opportunities. Here are but a few.

First is economic reform. Undoubtedly the task was immense in view of Russian mentality, and had never been attempted. If the process of "building socialism" has proved to be a failure everywhere, there is no guaranteed method for the "building of capitalism," especially on the ruins left behind by a regime whose main characteristic was a complete refusal of common sense solutions. Yet the experience of Germany in 1949 and 1990, as well as that of some other countries of Central Europe to a lesser extent, should provide two basic rules of conduct: (1) the most painful changes have to be brought about at the very start and as quickly as possible, for example the end of price fixing and the convertibility or currency; and (2) to do so it israte the changes in a consensual movement. political climate and to incorpoate the changes in a consensual movement

Gorbachev could avail himself of this climate of consensus in 1987, in 1988 undoubtedly, and probably up to the summer of 1989. However, it is questionable whether he was prevented from acting by an excessively conservative apparatus, especially at the government level, or whether—and may be concurrently—his grasp of economic problems was not sufficient and he allowed the opportunity to slip by.

At a plenum in the summer of 1987, after announcing a "radical reform" of the economy, he drew back as if overawed by the magnitude of the task, letting Prime Minister Ryzhkov take half measures, which only resulted in making problems worse. Towards the end of 1989 everyone noticed a sharp deterioration of an already shaky economic situation. In the spring of 1990 the new presidential regime was presented as the necessary condition for implementing the much delayed reform. But once again, nothing happened since the first meetings of the new Presidential Council ended in fresh postponements of decisions to be made in the autumn. Since the people no longer trusted either Gorbachev or any other authority under the impact of food shortages, it seems most unlikely that any measures taken can bring any improvement.

Another missed opportunity was the refining of relations between republics and the drafting a new "federation pact." From 1986, the start of the first nationalist clashes in Kazakhstan, and probably up to the summer of 1989, Mikhail Gorbachev was well able to give the country the new constitution he had promised from the beginning of *perestroika*. (In March 1986 the 27th Congress elected a constitutional commission under his chairmanship.) The new constitution could only be an improvement compared to the old one, and it promised to be well received by most of the republics. Only in 1989 did separatist movements gain ground, especially in the Baltic countries.

Once again Gorbachev failed to take any chances. Already his hesitation in the Karabakh affair, his refusal to come out in favor of autodetermination for the local population, deprived him of support among the Armenians, later the Azerbaidghanis, which ended with the whole Caucasus entering a stage of latent secession. Then it became clear with the Lithuanian CP declaration of independence in December 1989, and that of the republic itself in March 1990, that the autonomy movement was getting the upper hand. Henceforth the most docile republics will only accept deals which have been negotiated with their participation, not only with the Union—whose credibility is fast crumbling—but with individual republics, especially since the Russian federation, under Yeltsin, declared its willingness to enter into direct negotiations with other republics. The newly elected "President Gorbachev" saw his extended power shrink rapidly and to such an extent that some Soviet observers compare him to Perez de Quellar, the UNO General Secretary whose only mission is to act as go–between among sovereign states, unless it is more the case of a Lebanese presidential leadership with internecine quarrels between races and militias making it impossible to govern.

These two main "blunders" account for the drop in popularity of the father of *perestroika* in Russian public opinion. No doubt Gorbachev was more popular abroad than at home from the start, but the split became worse after the summer of 1989. While Eastern Europe was liberating itself (with Gorbachev taking much of credit for it in the West, mostly because he stood by), in the USSR itself *perestroika* entered a phase of stagnation at a time when a marked improvement in political pluralism and parliamentary life were not sufficient to counterbalance a worsening of the economic and nationality crisis.

To make matters worse for the Soviet leader, it was becoming increasingly more obvious that he did not have the legitimacy required under the new circumstances. He was elected Secretary General of the Party in the old fashion, then was appointed as head of state by successive parliaments, but he never went through the test of universal suffrage. In March 1989, another missed opportunity took place, for although he could have been elected easily in a constitutency, he preferred to follow his Politburo and enter parliament in the worst possible manner. He joined a list of a hundred people chosen by the Party Central Committee to be elected altogether. A year later, while it has been accepted that the President must be elected by universal suffrage, he decided that—in view of the "emergency"—the rule will not be applied this time. Mikhail Gorbachev was elected by members of the Congress only for five years with no credible competitor as countercandidate.

In other words, he became the leader without democratic rules. On the one hand, he ensured that the apparatus could not harm him by discarding the old regulations of cooperation, since as President of the USSR he can only be sacked by the Congress plenum, no longer by the "Presidium of the Supreme Soviet," which was a tool of the Politburo. Yet as Party leader he can no longer be dismissed by the Central Committee alone, as happened to Khrushchev in 1964; a new Congress has to be convened for this to take place. Meanwhile he managed to avoid an unavoidable component of all democratic regimes for a long time: universal suffrage. Therein lies the main difference, and his inferiority complex, vis-à-vis the electorate's darling Boris Yeltsin who was twice elected by popular vote (nearly 80 percent of the votes in Moscow and Sverdlovsk), he draws much benefit from this discrepancy. Or even vis-à-vis Ion Iliescu, a man who, under different circumstances and in good times, was elected by a wide majority as leader of an amended party–state in Romania.

For this reason the balance sheet of Gorbachev's rule is not so impressive as it was in 1987 when the book was completed. This was the most promising period of *perestroika*, not only because since that time problems have become so pressing as to seem insoluble but also because some weaknesses have appeared in the leader's character. He tends to ignore the hard realities of economic life, thinking problems can be solved with a few directives and instructions from the center. He finds it difficult to make decisions in the face difficult circumstances, which can be seen from the number of advisers he gathers around him. These "advisers," more or less radical in their ideas and disappointed in seeing their advice ignored, are eager to communicate their solutions to the media. Whereas a real statesman has few advisers who keep the lowest possible profile.

To this must be added an equally well known tendency to being authoritarian, which may be due in part to Raisa's strong influence as well as a taste for the trappings of power. To prove this point is the law passed in the spring of 1990 making attacks on the "president's prestige" punishable at his express demand. Another example was his unbending attitude toward Sakharov; there was a shameful clash at the Congress of Deputies between the President and the Academician only two days before the latter's death, which public opinion viewed as the reason for the death of the famous dissident. Other evidence can be found in the threats against Starkov, who was guilty of disrespect toward the President. The editor of *Arguments and Facts*, a highly popular weekly, is the only member of the press whose head Gorbachev would like to see roll for the simple reason that he published an opinion poll unfavorable to the Secretary General. There are also some recent events that have come to light: Boris Yeltsin's memoirs show that Gorbachev went blind with rage when he was criticized during a sitting of the Politburo in 1987, and he left the assembly for several minutes and returned without a word of apology.

This is not to say that the achievements are not there. Even more than Khrushchev—who has rightly been rehabilitated—Mikhail Gorbachev will be remembered in history as the man who gave new life to a fossilized system, who allowed Eastern Europe to recover her freedom, and the Germanies to be reunited, and the leader who put an end to costly foreign ventures and a vain military confrontation with the rest of the world. The only remaining question to answer is whether his achievements are not in the past and whether Gorbachev is the right man to preside over a crumbling empire and a system drifting into chaos. There probably is no recipe for miracles nor a savior to remedy such compounded difficulties. However, there is no standing still either since the USSR is engulfed in a revolutionary situation. It is a matter either of a leap forward to a genuine revolution and to introduce full democracy and a market economy, as some Eastern European countries have done, or it will be a leap backwards to the old dictatorship of the apparatus and the army, as it was in China.

Until now Gorbachev has refused the latter solution, but he has failed to choose the former, he appears to be applying the brakes rather than pushing forward with the necessary changes—and even worse, he clings to outmoded myths. Can be sincerely believe that communism as we have seen it so far can be reformed, or does at first have to come tumbling down altogether before a normal society can be build according to his wishes? If would be good to know that his hesitation is only tactical, that his references to Lenin are temporary, and that his aim is to take Russia into the international fold. However, there is no evidence that his main and ultimate aim is not personal power. Already from his five years in power one can be sure that if he has to choose between socialism and his remaining in power, he will certainly go for the latter. But if he has to choose between that and democracy, what will be his choice? It would be reassuring to know that this time it will not be personal power.

Let us hazard a guess. Sometime in 1991, or even later, the situation has become so chaotic that a delegation of high-ranking officers and top conservative officials meets the President to beg him to restore order. They have prepared a decree to declare a state of emergency in the republics most affected or even in the country as a whole. This emergency law was passed in the spring of 1990 and gave the President every power in the land; he can dissolve those parties or associations which are not to his liking, establish press censorship, requisition workers, and even suspend legal institutions such as parliaments and local governments. To be sure, this has to be endorsed by the Supreme Soviet of the USSR with a two-thirds majority in favor. However, will this obstacle be enough in the face of the army taking control of everything, putting pressure on reluctant deputies, or even arresting them? More to the point, how will President Gorbachev react when he is told that the decree is the only way to stop the army from acting independently, as well as keeping his power, especially if he is reminded that his prestige abroad can ensure that the West will prove understanding and allow a return to naked power, since he is the only person capable of explaining to Bush, Mitterand, and Major that the putsch is not illegal and that it is only a regrettable parenthesis on the way to *perestroika*. These are questions whose answers are all too potent to be brushed aside lightly.

NOTES

Notes to Chapter I

[1] *A Time for Peace* (New York: Richardson and Steirman,1985).
[2] See Zhorez Medvedev, *Gorbatchev* (Blackwell,1986), *passim*, especially data related to agriculture.
[3] Ibid.
[4] Ibid.
[5] *Otcherki Istorii Stavropolskoi organizatsii, KPSS* (Stavropol, 1970), p. 256.
[6] *Tchasovoi*, July–December 1950, *passim*.
[7] *Otcherki*, p. 382.
[8] Christian Schmidt–Hauer, *Michail Gorbatschow* (Piper, 1985), p. 65.

Notes to Chapter II

[1] *Pravda*, 20 May 1987.
[2] *Unita*, 9 April 1985.
[3] *L'Autre Europe*, no. 7/8, 1985.
[4] Ibid.
[5] Andrei Gromyko's preface to his speeches in *Safeguard the Peace on Our Planet* (Pergamon Press,1984).
[6] *Sovset News, The Electronic Newsletter of Soviet Studies*, II, No. 3, 19 June 1986.
[7] Ibid.
[8] Nikolai Poljanski and Alexander Rahr, *Gorbatschow, der neue Mann* (Universitas, 1986), *passim*.

Notes to Chapter III

[1] Dev Murarka, *Gorbatchev* (Ramsay, 1987), p. 65.
[2] *Pravda*, 12 January 1961.

[3] Cited by S.D. Ignatiev at the plenum of December 1958. Minutes, p. 337.

[4] *Pravda*, 31 January 1961.

[5] Khrushchev's speeches on agriculture, vol. 5, p. 423.

[6] *Otcherki*, p. 528.

[7] *L'Autre Europe*, no.7/8, 1985.

[8] Medvedev, *op. cit.*

[9] *Pravda*, 20 May 1987.

[10] *Pravda*, 10 April 1987.

[11] *Pravda*, 12 April 1987.

[12] *Stavropolskaia Pravda*, 6 May 1978.

[13] Murarka, *op. cit.* p. 99.

Notes to Chapter IV

[1] Arkadi Chevtchenko, *Rupture avec Moscou* (Payot, 1985), *passim*.

[2] See Medvedev, *op. cit.*, pp. 110–116.

[3] Murarka, *op. cit.*, p. 131.

[4] Minutes of the 27th Congress, vol. 3.

[5] See catalog of deputies of the Supreme Soviet of the RSFSR for 1987.

[6] Documents of the extraordinary plenum of the CC PCUS, *Politizdat*, March 1985.

Notes to Chapter V

[1] *Pravda*, 26 February 1986.

[2] *Pravda*, 28 January 1987.

[3] Ibid.

[4] Ibid.

[5] Version published by Radio Liberty, Munich.

[6] *Pravda*, 28 January 1987.

[7] Ibid.

[8] *Pravda*, 24 April 1985.

[9] *Pravda*, 12 June 1985.

[10] *Pravda*, 2 September 1985; *Time*, 9 September 1985.

[11] *Party Life*, no. 16, August 1986.

[12] *Pravda*, 28 January 1987.

[13] *Party Life*, no. 19, October 1986.

[14] *Pravda*, 28 January 1987.

[15] *Supra*, note 11.

[16] *Pravda,* 15 July 1987.
[17] *Pravda,* 28 January 1987.
[18] *Pravda,* 17 April 1987.
[19] *Perestroika,* p. 31.
[20] *Pravda,* 24 April 1985.
[21] *Komunist,* no. 9, June 1985.
[22] *Tass,* 25 February 1986.
[23] Ibid.
[24] Ibid.
[25] *Party Life,* no. 13, July 1987.
[26] Ibid.
[27] *Izvestia,* 20 November 1986.
[28] *Party Life,* no. 8, April 1986.

Notes to Chapter VI

[1] *Pravda,* 4 June 1987.
[2] *Pravda,* 30 January 1987.
[3] *Pravda,* 28 January 1987.
[4] *Pravda,* 14 February 1987.
[5] *Partiinaia Jizn,* no. 19, October 1986.
[6] *L'Humanité,* 12 June 1987.
[7] *Komunist,* no. 4, March 1987.
[8] The electronic Newsletter of Soviet Studies, CSIS, Georgetown University, vol. III, no. 1, January 27, 1987.

Notes to Chapter VII

[1] *Voprosy Istorii KPSS,* no. 1, January 1987.
[2] *Literaturnaia Gazeta,* 24 June 1986.
[3] Murarka, *op. cit.*
[4] *Pravda,* 2 February 1986.
[5] *Pravda Vostoka,* 7 June 1986.
[6] *Pravda,* 28 February 1986.
[7] *Pravda,* 28 August 1986.
[8] *Izvestia,* 4 June 1987.
[9] *Partiinaia Jizn,* no. 5, March 1986.
[10] *Le Monde,* 16 July 1986.
[11] *Pravda,* 9 February 1986.
[12] *Pravda,* 20 March 1987.
[13] *Partiinaia Jizn,* no. 12, June 1985.

[14] *Sovietskaia Moldavia*, 22 October 1986.

[15] *Partiinaia Jizn*, no. 18, September 1986.

[16] *Pravda*, 25 March 1987.

[17] *Pravda*, 28 January 1987.

[18] Ibid.

[19] *Pravda*, 29 January 1987.

[20] Tass, 26 June 1987.

[21] *Sovietskaia Rossia*, 10 February 1987.

[22] *Pravda*, 13 February 1986.

[23] *Pravda*, 27 February 1986.

[24] *Komunist*, no. 13, September 1986.

[25] *Pravda*, 14 February 1987.

[26] *Pravda*, 20 May 1987.

Notes to Chapter VIII

[1] *Partiinaia Jizn*, no. 8, April 1986.

[2] *Pravda*, 17 June 1986.

[3] Extracts from speech of 19 June 1986 distributed by Radio Liberty.

[4] *Partiinaia Jizn*, no. 19, October 1986.

[5] Ibid.

[6] *Pravda*, 17 April 1987.

[7] *Pravda*, 31 July 1986.

[8] *Supra*, note 4.

[9] *Komunist*, no. 4, March 1987.

[10] Ibid.

[11] *New Times*, no. 5, February 1987.

[12] *Pravda*, 3 November 1987.

[13] *Pravda*, 31 July 1986.

[14] *Literaturnaia Rossia*, 27 March 1987.

[15] See the monthly supplement of *Komsomolskaia Pravda*, 23 May 1987; *International Herald Tribune*, 25 May 1987; *Times* (London), 3 June 1987; and, especially, the account distributed by *La Pensée Russe à Paris* dated 31 July 1987.

[16] *Pravda*, 27 January 1987.

[17] *International Herald Tribune*, 2 April 1987.

Notes to Chapter IX

[1] 1. See chapter 8, note 3.

2 *International Herald Tribune*, 2 April 1987.
3 *Pravda*, 8 January 1987.
4 *Pravda*, 29 January 1987.
5 *Pravda*, 31 May 1987.
6 *Krasnaia Zvezda*, 17 June 1987.
7 *Krasnaia Zvezda*, 18 March 1987.
8 *Pravda*, 11 July 1985.
9 Tass, 19 July 1986.